IMAGES
of America

HIGHLANDS

This aerial view of Highlands, taken from an airplane above Lake Sequoyah Dam on January 12, 1972, shows the town of Highlands (top left) flanked by Satulah and Fodderstack Mountains on the right and the base of Big Bear Pen Mountain on the left. To the right is Highlands Country Club, and at left are Mirror Lake and its bridge. (Photograph by Dick Dillon.)

ON THE COVER: Photographed in 1897–1898 by Henry Scadin, Highlands House was built in 1880 as the town's first hotel. Its builder, Maj. Joseph Halleck, was Union general Henry Halleck's brother. It quickly became a mecca for summer lodgers, the number of guests in 1883 —409—exceeding the town's population—300—by a third. The National Register of Historic Places lists it as Highlands Inn. (Photograph from the Harbison Collection.)

IMAGES
of America

HIGHLANDS

Dr. Randolph Preston Shaffner

ARCADIA
PUBLISHING

Published by Arcadia Publishing
Charleston, South Carolina

Library of Congress Catalog Card Number: 2008920186

For all general information contact Arcadia Publishing at:
Telephone 843-853-2070
Fax 843-853-0044
E-mail sales@arcadiapublishing.com
For customer service and orders:
Toll-Free 1-888-313-2665

Visit us on the Internet at www.arcadiapublishing.com

This book is dedicated to the people of Highlands and its surroundings who have preserved and continue to preserve their family photographs for future generations.

CONTENTS

ACKNOWLEDGMENTS

Since the Highlands Historical Society was founded in 1979 and reactivated in 1999, hundreds of volunteers have contributed tens of thousands of hours toward preserving and promoting the history of Highlands and its surrounding plateau. It is impossible to thank all those volunteers individually, but without their hard work and their love of local history, much of this book would not have been possible.

The book's images have now been incorporated into the Highlands Historical Society's archives. They were supplied by generous families of the town and the surrounding area as well as relatives and descendants from across the United States. The accompanying historical texts were distilled from oral interviews and family scrapbooks, photo albums, memoirs, diaries, documents, deeds, histories, genealogies, and letters.

Additional historical information was gleaned from such publications as my own *Good Reading Material, Mostly Bound and New: The Hudson Library, 1884–1994* (1994) and *Heart of the Blue Ridge: Highlands, North Carolina*, 2nd edition (2004); the Macon County Historical Society's *Heritage of Macon County, North Carolina*, Volumes 1 (1987) and 2 (1998); John Preston Arthur's *Western North Carolina, A History, 1730–1913* (1914); E. E. Ewing's "History of the Settlement of Highlands," *Blue Ridge Enterprise*, January 25, 1883; Helen Hill Norris's *Looking Backward*, Volumes 1 (1961) and 2 (1963); Carol Carré Perrin's *Highlands Historic Inventory: Project Completion Report* (1982); T. W. Reynolds's *High Lands* (1964) and *Southern Appalachian Region*, Volumes 1 and 2 (1966); and Ralph M. Sargent's *Biology in the Blue Ridge: Fifty Years of the Highlands Biological Station, 1927–1977* (1977).

Special appreciation is extended to all those individuals named as contributors of photographs in this volume.

I also wish to thank Maggie Bullwinkel, acquisitions editor, and Mike Litchfield and Barbie Halaby, production editors, at Arcadia Publishing for their help and assistance with this project.

And finally, to my wife, Margaret, whose deep love of Highlands and its people were the inspiration for this book, I extend my appreciation for her devoted support, not just on this project, but in everything!

I hope this volume encourages the rediscovery and sharing of forgotten photographs in family closets, attics, and basements throughout the Highlands plateau.

INTRODUCTION

I look across to Highlands Falls
And hear the water roar,
It seems to me a voice that calls
From all time gone before.

—Highlands native Christina Anderson Rice, 1923

This little book focuses only on the 55 years before and after the founding of the village of Highlands, North Carolina—that is to say, from 1820 to 1930. Many people and events had to be omitted either because of the unavailability of photographs or the inherent restraints of a small book, but every effort was made to provide a representative cross-sampling of the extraordinary variety of people who contributed to the early history of the town and its surroundings.

Although the Highlands plateau was created 350 million years ago on the crest of the world's oldest mountains, the village of Highlands was founded in 1875 by two developers living in Kansas. According to legend, they took a map in hand and drew a line from New York to New Orleans, then passed another line between Chicago and Savannah. These lines, they predicted, would be the great trade routes of the future, and where they crossed would someday be a great population center.

What evolved was a health and summer resort at more than 4,000 feet on the highest crest of the western North Carolina plateau in the southern Appalachian Mountains. This paradisical settlement, the highest incorporated town east of the Rockies, provided common ground for both Northern and Southern pioneers a decade after their great Civil War. By 1883, nearly 300 emigrants from the Eastern states were calling Highlands home.

In the early 1880s, the town contained eight country stores specializing in groceries, hardware, and general merchandise; a post office; a hotel and a boardinghouse for summer guests; a public library; four churches (Presbyterian, Episcopal, Baptist, and Methodist); and a first-class school.

Very little changed in the town until the late 1920s, when the Cullasaja River was dammed to form Lake Sequoyah, providing hydroelectric power. A spectacularly scenic road from Highlands toward Franklin was carved into the rock walls of the Cullasaja Gorge, and the muddy roads in and out of town were reinforced with crushed stone. By the time the chamber of commerce was established in 1931, the town's population had increased to 500, with 2,500 to 3,000 summer guests and 25 businesses.

Again, very little changed from the 1930s through the 1960s. Highlands missed the Great Depression because most of its residents were accustomed to surviving hard times, growing their own meat and vegetables so that no one went hungry. Entertainment was homegrown, the most popular pastimes being square dancing, buck dancing, and mountain clogging. For 50 years, Helen's Barn was the great equalizer, amalgamating winter and summer residents alike into a single class of foot-stomping revelers swinging to the twangs and whines of banjos and fiddles.

Occasionally the circus climbed the mountain to Highlands, but always open were Anderson's Five and Ten or Doc Mitchell's Drug Store on Fourth Street Hill and Bill's Soda Shop at Fourth and Main Streets, serving creamy milk shakes, sandwiches, cherry smashes, and ammonia Cokes.

The mid-1970s saw the sudden influx of multifamily homes and shopping centers that spawned land-use plans and zoning laws intended to protect Highlands' natural assets. For the most part, the shops have remained individual. Chain stores have not yet robbed the village of its differences from the "Xeroxed" American town. The town's population today stands at 958 year-round residents, with 15,000 to 20,000 summer guests and 387 businesses.

Since its founding in 1875, the demographic mixture of Highlands has been remarkably unique. Founded by hardy pioneers from across the nation, sober industrious tradesmen from the North, Scotch-Irish laborers and craftsmen from the surrounding mountains and valleys, and wealthy aristocratic planters and professionals from the South, the town has served as a cultural center for well-known artists, musicians, actors, authors, photographers, scholars, and scientists who have thrived in its natural setting.

The result is a town too cosmopolitan to be provincial, too broadly based to be singular in attitude and perspective, too enamored of its natural surroundings to be totally indifferent to them, and just isolated enough and small enough to be anxious about the benefits and setbacks of growth and development.

Oh, how it is a man may grow
Away from his own soul—
How Nature kindly takes him back
And gently makes him Whole.

—Highlands native Bess Hines Harkins, 1959

One of the most popular overviews of Highlands, North Carolina, is from Sunset Rock, which the children of Prioleau and Margaretta Ravenel donated to the town in 1914 in loving memory of their parents. In conjunction with the purchase and preservation of the top of Satulah Mountain in 1909, these were the beginnings of today's Highlands Land Trust. (Photograph by Cynthia Strain, October 31, 1999.)

One

BOTANICAL PARADISE

A primeval forest once extended from Bear Pen to Whiteside Mountains. It contained 1,900 acres of giant Carolina and Canadian hemlocks, oaks, silverbells, cherry birches, Fraser magnolias, and cucumber trees, including the largest chokecherry tree in the world. This region of undisturbed forest was once recognized in its perfection by William Coker as "the most magnificent growth east of the Mississippi." (Photograph from Ann Wotten and Louise Rideout Beacham.)

Henry Wright stands in the Richardson Woods beside a typical oak that was 8 feet in diameter and 150 feet tall. This forest took a millennium to grow but disappeared in just a handful of years. Sold in 1943 for the war effort, it was decimated by 1948, representing a huge loss for those who knew and loved it. (Photograph by George Masa from Beverly Cook Quin.)

This slab of Eastern hemlock (*Tsuga canadensis*) from Munger Creek was cut for the new Highlands Estates—today's country club—and donated by its president, Scott Hudson, to the Highlands Museum in 1928. Displaying 439 rings, the tree was a sapling of three years when Columbus set sail for America. A 450-year-old slab of white oak (*Quercus alba*) from the same primeval forest is also displayed at the nature center. (Photograph by the author.)

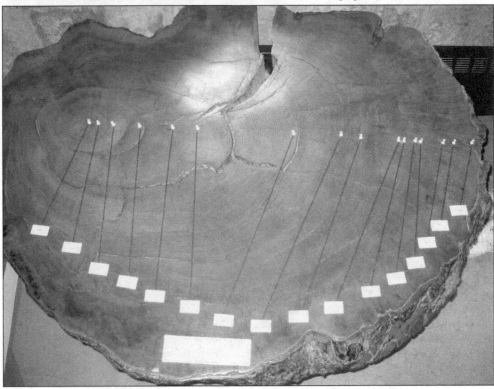

Whiteside, known to Cherokees as *Unaka Kanoos* (White Mountain or White Bear), is one of the world's oldest mountains, figured from its half-billion-year-old parent rock that was exposed during the last continental collision. Named for the reflecting whiteness of feldspar, quartz, and mica in its southeastern face, it was called by Edward King "one of the sublimest natural monuments in the United States," a 2,000-foot petrified waterfall. (Photograph from Harbison Collection.)

Devil's Courthouse is a dome-shaped rock at the north end of Whiteside Mountain that the Cherokees called *Inda-culla*. The Europeans often named this type of inaccessible rock after the extreme difficulty involved in penetrating thickets and scaling boulders to reach the top. From such dizzying heights, the devil might very well have hurled his victims into the great abyss below. (Photograph by Henry Scadin from Bascom Estate.)

Clovis Fluted Point
9000 - 10000 B. C.

Hardaway Dalton
8000 - 8500 B. C.

Fluted Point
9000 B. C.

Graver
8000 - 9000 B. C.

End Scrapers
7000 - 10000 B. C.

Spokeshave
8000 - 9000 B. C.

William B. Cleaveland collected over 2,500 Native American artifacts, including beautifully carved arrowheads, pottery etched with Cherokee history, primitive tomahawks, and peace pipes, some dating back 10,000 years to the Archaic and Woodland periods, as identified by Dan and Phyllis Morse at the nature center. In 1886, Cleaveland's advertisement for his grocery store offered "Indian Relics taken in exchange for goods." (Photograph by the author.)

It was not the Spanish conquistadors but the great English, French, and American botanists who appreciated the unspoiled beauty of these upper mountains. William Bartram (1729–1823), son of American botanist John Bartram (1699–1777), explored the southern Appalachians, passing through the Vale of Cowee—modern Macon County—in the spring of 1776, as described in his *Travels*. (Portrait by Charles Willson Peale, c. 1808, from Independence National Historical Park.)

The French botanist André Michaux (1746–1802) made the first of several journeys into the "high mountains of Carolina" in 1787, where he discovered the rare plant *Shortia galacifolia* and on June 16 crossed over Wildcat Gap on the Highlands plateau. Michaux's son, François André (1770–1855), right, assisted his father on his journeys and pursued his own classic study of American forests. (Photograph from Rueben Goldthwaites's *Early Western Travels*.)

America's leading botanist in the mid-19th century, Asa Gray (1810–1888), visited several times from 1838 to 1879 trying to rediscover Michaux's long-lost *Shortia*. Gray's *Manual of the Botany of the Northern United States* became the standard American field guide. His discovery of close affinities between East Asian and North American flora was a key piece of evidence in support of Darwin's theory of evolution. (Photograph from Harvard University Herbaria Collection.)

As early as 1839, Silas McDowell guided North Carolina botanist Dr. Moses Ashley Curtis (1808–1872) to High Falls, also known as Cullasaja, Pitcher, or Dry Falls. *Scribner's* journalist Edward King (1848–1896) visited and sketched "Dry Fall of the Sugar Fork" (upper left) in 1873 for his book *The Great South*. He marveled at how the entire river flung itself in a passionate leap over a great escarpment of gray bare rocks, leaving anyone who passed under it essentially dry. The photographs taken in 1890 (upper right) and 1883 (below), the latter by John Bundy, are only two of thousands snapped by awestruck visitors to the site over the past century and a half. (Sketch by Edward King; upper photograph from Tom Crumpler Collection; lower photograph from Hudson Library Collection.)

Flowing over Dry Falls is the Cullasaja River, pronounced *Cull-uh-say-jah* and named by the Cherokees *Kûlsetsiy*. It meant literally "honey-locust place," but Europeans, adopting the nearest English equivalent, called it Sugar Town, meaning the place where sugar trees grew. Several miles below Dry Falls, the Cullasaja pours over a giant 100-foot staircase of several falls, also sketched in 1873 by King in his *The Great South*. (Drawing from *The Great South*.)

Washington Irving called Michigan-born writer and landscape artist Charles Lanman (1819–1895) "the picturesque explorer of our country." As early as 1848, Lanman visited the Highlands plateau and described an impressive cataract that he called Sugar Water Falls. Known today as Lower Cullasaja Falls, this cascade was photographed by Henry Scadin in 1898. Barely visible (lower left) are Barak and Margaret Phillips Wright in Sunday attire. (Photograph from Hudson Library Collection.)

Long before a spectacularly scenic Highway 28 was constructed through the Cullasaja River Gorge to link Highlands with Franklin in 1928–1929, a Cherokee trail passed near the top of the mountain under Bridal Veil Falls, which the highway would follow as well. It wasn't until 1958–1961 that a 28/64 bypass allowed drivers the choice of going under the river or around it. (Photograph by George Masa from Beverly Cook Quin.)

The Cherokees called the three large cascades that plunged 400 feet down Overflow Creek Ahmihcahlahlagah Falls. In 1883, Jonathan Heacock built a dam and sawmill near the headwaters of this creek and renamed the cascades Glen Falls, after one of the lovely waterfalls in his home state of Pennsylvania. Alternative names have been Omakaluka, Oumekeloke, and Overflow Falls. (Photograph from *Beyond Satulah Lies Highlands*, published by Highlands Chamber of Commerce.)

Just below the dam, which in 1927 impounded a new 70-acre Lake Sequoyah in order to furnish Highlands with its first hydroelectric power, Cullacaleski (also spelled Kalakalaski) Falls stair-stepped down 220 feet to a power plant. This plant provided the potential for 900 horsepower and would light and supply the town for the next 40 years. (Photograph by R. Henry Scadin, 1898, from Special Collections, UNC–Asheville.)

Waterfalls have always been a prime attraction in the mountains, despite the dangers that they pose for unwary visitors. A number of unfortunate sightseers ranging in age from 9 to 38 have lost their lives falling from Dry Falls, Glen Falls, Secret Falls, and even the 150-foot Picklesimer Falls downstream from this view of Satulah Falls on the south slope of Satulah Mountain. (Photograph by the author.)

The waterfall that Michaux must have seen after crossing Wildcat Gap was lovely Highlands Falls, which once plunged amidst towering hemlocks in the primeval forest but now graces the 16th green of Highlands Falls Country Club. Local poet Christina Rice described the roaring water of Highlands Falls as "a voice that called from all time gone before." (Photograph by Henry Scadin, 1898, from Harbison Collection.)

Pinkerton Pool Falls, reached only by a winding path off the Cashiers road to the Cullasaja River where it first crosses the highway, was once in the public domain but is now private. It became a favorite swimming hole for picnicking Highlanders, and children ran through the hollow thunderstruck tripod birch that stood by its path. (Photograph by Henry Scadin, 1897, from *Highlands House* brochure.)

Two

PREHISTORY

It was Silas McDowell (1795–1879), a self-educated geologist, mineralogist, zoologist, and botanical explorer and guide from Franklin, North Carolina, who first promoted what he called the Sugartown Highlands in the 1840s. He envisioned the plateau as a health and summer resort without equal in the South, and his articles in *Smithsonian Reports* and various horticultural publications eventually attracted town founders Samuel Kelsey and C. C. Hutchinson. (Photograph from Macon County Historical Society.)

Even before the Cherokees departed on their Trail of Tears, hearty pioneers were already settling the Sugartown Highlands plateau. Among the first were David Rogers (1790–1882) and Martha "Patsy" Young Rogers (1792–1873), both from Washington County, Tennessee, who arrived in 1820. The Rogers home, which still stands today in the Buck Creek community, was the setting for the Hallmark television production of *Foxfire* in 1992. (Photograph from Frances Crunkleton Wright.)

In 1844, gold miner Joseph W. Dobson (born 1815), a Haywood County native, and Rebecca Ogilvie Dobson (born 1817) purchased State Grants 1084 and 1085—640 acres where Highlands would later exist—for 10¢ an acre. Their son, William B. Dobson (1852–1930), and his wife, Mary E. Dobson (1851–1908), would inherit the tracts, selling them to Kelsey and Hutchinson in 1875 for $2 an acre. (Photograph by the author of gravestone in Cartoogechaye.)

In 1848, Hugh "Huey" Gibson (born 1824), a cooper, and Mary Ann Gibson (born 1832) bought 100 acres at 5¢ per acre on Sugartown Creek but lived in a single-room log cabin near today's Catholic church, caretaking Dobson's apple orchard and cattle. The rock, where salt was spread to calm the stock during summers, still exists at today's Wright Square. (Drawing from Richard Harding Davis's *By-Paths in the Mountains*, 1876.)

Isaac N. Keener (1811–1889) and Polly Jennings Keener (1819–1898) came up the mountain from Ellijay in 1850 and bought a state grant at Gold Mine Bridge. Among their 11 children was Brownlow Keener (1851–1936), pictured with his wife, Martha Carolina Holland (1854–1919). Brownlow and Martha had 13 children, from whom many Highlanders today are descended. Many Keeners are buried at Miller Cemetery. (Photograph from Frances Crunkleton Wright.)

The Highlands ridge known as Billy Cabin was named for Billy Webb (1829–1905), who came from Cocke County, Tennessee, around 1850–1852. There were eight children by his first wife, Mary Polly Giles Webb (1818–1888) in Tennessee, and 13 children by his second wife, Lucretia "Granny Creasy" Gibson Webb (1835–1916) in Highlands, making the Webb genealogy a veritable web of Webbs. Billy and Creasy are seated. (Photograph from Reba Talley Webb.)

Billy and Creasy's second home, a double log cabin joined by a dogtrot, was at Flat Mountain. From left to right in 1915 are (seated) Mary McCall Webb and Ruthie McCall Webb; (standing) Cindy McCall Webb and daughter Lindy Webb. Billy built his third home when the town was founded in 1875 and is buried there near today's Brushy Face Road. (Photograph by Mary Lapham from Hudson Library Collection.)

The "Old Highlands Hunter," who migrated from Tuckasegee to Clear Creek in December 1851, was Gabriel Benson Picklesimer (1818–1904). He first married Nancy McCall (1828–1863) and then Mary A. Elizabeth Thompson (1839–1925), fathering altogether 18 children. His own father, blacksmith and gunsmith Abraham Picklesimer (1787–1861), had 12 children, so there are many Picklesimer descendants living in Highlands today. (Photograph by Henry Scadin, November 17, 1899, from Irene Picklesimer James.)

John C. Wilson (1812–1884) and Elizabeth Henderson Wilson (born 1813), from Buncombe County, homesteaded at today's landfill south of Fodderstack Mountain before Wilson bought the land in 1858. In 1869, his estate of 550 acres, including Henson Queen's Mountain, was valued at 85¢ an acre, which his son Asbel Madison "Mack" Wilson (1840–1923) and Elizabeth Ann "Betsy Ann" Brown Wilson (1842–1932), pictured below, inherited. (Photograph from Neville Wilson.)

Before Highlands existed, James "Jim" Dorran Russell (1833–1900), a native of Macon County, had built a home in 1853 at Broadway Gap on today's Dillard Road. Around 1867, about the time he married John Arnold's sister, Elizabeth Arnold (1844–1910), his first cousin William Ganaway Russell (1835–1921) and Jane Nicholson Russell (1851–1935) of Oconee, South Carolina, (pictured above) were building a stage stop and inn to provide overnight lodging for weary travelers between the train station in Walhalla, South Carolina, and the mountain resort area around Highlands. Listed on the National Register as the Russell House, this popular farmstead accommodated as many as 80 overnight lodgers at a time in addition to 17 Russell children. Until it burned in 1988, it stood on the bank of the Chattooga River. (Photographs from the Oconee Heritage Center.)

Pryor Talley (born around 1819–1822) of Pendleton, South Carolina, and Cloah "Cloey" Burrell Talley (born 1825) of Pine Mountain, Georgia, built a cabin, shown around 1910, near Shortoff Mountain in 1855. In 1868, they sold it to James Wright (1811–1886) of Greenville, Tennessee, and Jemima Norton Wright (1816–1897), pictured at upper right in her 70s. James Wright (upper left, in his 20s) willed it to Barak Wright (1847–1926) for "the love and affection he has for his son" in 1872, reserving lifetime use. Barak expanded it around 1920, and around 1950, his grandson Chester tore it down, rebuilding it as it exists today. The home fronts U.S. 64, once called the Norton Road or "the Lane." (Upper photographs from Frances Crunkleton Wright; lower photograph from Linda Wright David.)

Elias Norton's widow, Mary "Polly" Holden Norton (1816–1897), upper left, moved with her seven children from Whiteside Cove to Shortoff around 1859. Her son-in-law Isaac "Peter" Rice (1836–1914) built for her a 12-room house around an original log and wide-plank cabin set back from the road amid apple trees, a hemlock hedge, and a stone wall across the front. Here, for 65 years, Polly's daughter Elizabeth Vinetta "Nettie" Norton Rice (1842–1928), upper right, operated Idlease, a boardinghouse, for income. Nettie served guests fresh vegetables from her garden. She had 11 children, whom she reared alone after Peter headed west to seek his fortune. Her daughter Darthula "Sula" Rice (1867–1945) managed Idlease for 17 years until her own death. The house still stands at the corner of Buck Creek Road and Cheney Lane. (Photographs from Tammy Lowe.)

Miller Cemetery exists about where Joseph John Miller (1790–1880) and Susanna "Susan" Tabitha Grant Miller (c. 1816–1886) came from Cowee Creek to live during the early 1860s. Miller had 20 or more children, 12 by a previous marriage to Sarah Cox (1794–c. 1835). His grandson David Hiram Miller (1865–1944) and Rachel Louise Henderson Miller (1868–1935) are shown plowing with children, from left to right, Noah (age five), Lola (age seven), and Ethel (age two). (Photograph by Henry Scadin, March 23, 1897, from Hudson Library Collection.)

Henry Scadin's charming photograph of three more of Joseph's and Sarah's great-grandchildren, taken on May 7, 1897, features (from left to right) Jemima "Mima" Miller (born 1891), who married Dewitt Ransom Bryson in 1908 and lived in Brevard; Ulysses (born 1892), who was killed in action in World War I; and Carlton (born 1893), who was killed by a falling wall in Rosman in 1920. (Photograph from Hudson Library Collection.)

Felix Kilpatrick (1815–1908) and Sousan Pruett Kilpatrick (1820–1897) built a cabin at Dog Mountain in 1860. In 1881, Robert "Bob" David Rogers (born 1832) and Judith Caroline Holland Rogers (1834–1907) bought it. After their son Noah married Laura Miller, it became known as the Laura Rogers house until Col. John Sewell's caretakers, the Earl Crunkletons, made it their home in 1927. It was dismantled in 2000. (Photograph from Highlands Historic Inventory.)

Highlands's first teacher, John Newton Arnold (1840–1936) of Macon County, and Althia Ledford Arnold (1849–1932) bought 100 acres between Dog Mountain and Dry Falls in 1874. A highly honored Confederate veteran, Arnold fought at various times under Generals Lee, Jackson, and Stuart and spent a year and a half in prison camps. He taught a four-month curriculum at Billy Cabin in 1875. (Photograph by the author of gravestone at Sugarfork Baptist Church.)

Three

1875–1900

A well-known legend of the founding of Highlands claims that two developers living in Kansas took a map in hand and drew a line from New York to New Orleans. Then they passed another line between Chicago and Savannah. These lines, they predicted, would be the great trade routes of the future, and where they crossed would someday be a great population center. (Drawing from the booklet *Highlands, N.C.*, 1956.)

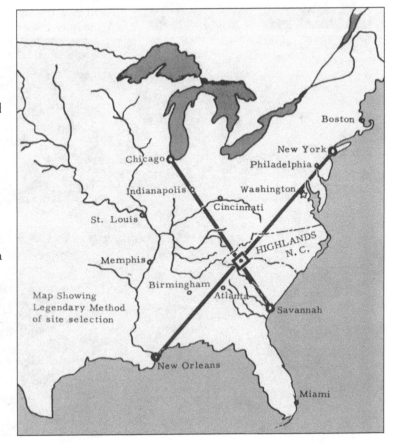

Map Showing Legendary Method of site selection

A native of the village of Florida, New York, and a founder of several towns, Samuel Truman Kelsey (1832–1921) chose the forested mountains of North Carolina to establish the first summer resort in the Blue Ridge. At 4,000 feet, Highlands became the highest incorporated town in eastern America. Kelsey lived with his wife, Katherine "Katy" E. Ricksecker Kelsey (born c. 1844), daughter Laura, and sons Truman, Harlan, and Harry. (Photograph from Sky Campbell.)

Kelsey's home, built in 1875, had a central hall, parlor, living room, and dining room downstairs with a wing containing a butler's pantry, a kitchen, and a back porch. Upstairs housed three bedrooms with two large closets. The total building cost was $350. It would have been the oldest house in Highlands had it not burned to the ground in 1976, only the dry-laid stone chimney remaining. (Photograph from Highlands Community Theatre Collection.)

A native of Bernard, Vermont, Clinton Carter "C. C." Hutchinson (1833–1909) was also a founder of towns. On March 6, 1875, he borrowed $1,678 to buy one and a third square miles at $2 an acre. In 1879, however, he left Highlands with his wife, Gertrude Harriet Sherman Hutchinson (born 1851), son Reno, and daughter Gertrude, having only begun his new home across Main Street from Kelsey's residence. (Photograph from the *Highlander* newspaper.)

The foundation of Hutchinson's home, built from giant oak trees split lengthwise and dropped into 8-foot, rock-lined trenches, was intended to "last till doomsday," according to Dr. Charles Frost, who finished Hutchinson's house with massive, hand-squared, white pine logs, placed upright, and walls weatherboarded inside and clapboarded outside to avoid the rough appearance of a stockade. Even in the strongest winds, the home never trembled. (Photograph from Highlands Historic Inventory.)

Responding to Kelsey's brochure, T. Baxter White (1834–1922) and Eleanor Clark Barber White (born 1836) arrived in July 1875 from Marblehead, Massachusetts, as Highlands's first settlers. White served as Highlands's first postmaster and as justice of the peace, councilman, and the longest-serving trustee of the library. He wrote the "Highlands" column for the *Franklin Press*, the only link the little mountain town had with the outside world. (Photograph from the Bascom Estate.)

White built his home (right) on the south side of Main Street, which also served as post office and country store, offering groceries, dry and canned goods, boots, shoes, galoshes, hats, notions, and stationery. He touted the natural taste of his evaporated peaches and pears and the high quality of his teas and coffee. The Whites left for California in 1911. (Photograph by Henry Scadin from Doris Potts.)

Farmer George Alexander Jacobs (1840–1921) from Jefferson County, Tennessee, and Mary "Mollie" Jane Temple Wolf Jacobs (1842–1917), a widow from England, built Highlands's first boardinghouse at First and Main Streets in the fall of 1875. It was later home to Robert Reese, then Jim Rogers. Jacobs was Highlands's first justice of the peace and first appointed mayor from 1879 to 1883. He managed Annie Dimick's Cheap Cash Store on Main Street. (Photograph from Dallas Reese Jr.)

According to E. E. Ewing, only four homes existed in Highlands at the end of 1876: those of Kelsey, White, Jacobs, and Yankee farmer James Benson Soper (1836–1911) from Union Township, Pennsylvania, and Elizabeth Gustin Soper (1839–1898). The Sopers returned to Pennsylvania in 1881. After 1932, their farmstead, situated on 100 acres off today's Flat Mountain Road, was home to Frazier and Ethel Redden. (Photograph by the author.)

John Palmer "Dock" McKinney (1854–1938), grandson of James McKinney, who settled Cashiers Valley, and Margaret "Jane" Gribble McKinney (1854–1935) arrived at the beginning of 1876 and lived on Fourth Street north of town. They built their own home in 1898 on Chestnut Street at the site of today's performing arts center. Their son Allison "Al" Dickerson McKinney was reportedly the first child born in the new town on November 18, 1876 (unless it was William McHenry Jackson, for whom no date is given). Jane Gribble's mother, Claressa Louise Adeline Gribble (1827–1907), was a Cherokee who was 12 years old when she was sent on the Trail of Tears march to Oklahoma, but she had trouble keeping up, and Clark and Polly Rogers took her in as a foster child. (Photographs from Jessie Potts Owens.)

John Norton (1849–1924), son of Elias and Polly Norton and married to Sibbie Elizabeth Dockins (born 1860), bought both sides of West Main Street and built Central House, Highlands's second boardinghouse, in 1877–1878. In 1880, he traded it for Joseph Halleck's newly built Highlands House (Highlands Inn). He was one of Highlands's first appointed commissioners from 1879 to 1883 and moved to Cullowhee around 1905–1907. (Photograph from Tammy Lowe.)

Norton's Central House, a two-and-a-half-story frame structure with gabled roof and a two-tier front porch, had 11 bedrooms, no plumbing or electricity, water piped from Satulah Mountain, and a four-hole outhouse, two for each sex. It was managed by Joseph Halleck from 1880 to 1888, David and Mattie Norton from 1888 to 1904, Billy and Mattie Potts from 1905 to 1914, and Minnie Edwards until the early 1950s. (Photograph by John Bundy, 1883.)

Arthur T. House (born 1845) and Sarah F. Bidwell House (born 1852) of Hartford, Connecticut, built their home, according to E. E. Ewing, "at the opening of 1877." Currently the oldest house in Highlands, it serves as Highlands Historical Society's living history museum. On Mill Creek, House constructed the first sawmill within the town, and he also built Highlands's first school. He and Sarah returned to Connecticut around 1882. (Photograph by the author.)

The descendants of house painter Charles Benson Edwards (1848–1894?) of Milledgeville, Georgia, and Sarah Leatha Edwards (1857–1929) of Horse Cove still occupy their original family homestead. The Edwards family built a home and barn at the end of Fifth Street in 1878, replacing it with a Queen Anne–style cottage around 1891. When Charles Edwards, seeking work, disappeared in 1894, his son, Grover, supported the bereaved family. (Photograph from Highlands Historic Inventory.)

Stanhope Walker "Squire" Hill (1815–1894) and Celia Marinda Edwards Hill (1819–1888) came from Horse Cove in July 1878 to live in the house their son, Frank, built for them at Sixth and Main Streets, including a cabin for former slave Dan, who had remained with them after Emancipation. Hill became Highlands's first elected mayor in 1883 but returned to Horse Cove two years later. (Photograph from Luther Turner.)

The Hill House accommodated early Highlands settlers as boarders. It existed on one of Hill's greatest legacies: the road to Horse Cove, which he surveyed along an old Cherokee trail. Swiss professor Albert Staub (born 1830) and daughter, Albertina, arriving in 1887, occupied the Hill House while Albert taught at the Highlands Academy and Albertina ran the library and sold real estate and insurance. (Photograph from Highlands Historic Inventory.)

Highlands's first resident doctor was Dr. George Washington Kibbee (1822–1878) from Litchfield, Connecticut, who, with Laura Almira Grosvenor Kibbee (1830–1911), built a home at Satulah's base in 1878. A specialist at treating specific fevers, he departed to treat yellow fever victims in New Orleans and died saving others. His daughter, Laura "Kittie" Kibbee (1863–1947) taught school and was Highlands's first librarian. From 1920 to 1976, the Kibbee house was known as Chestnut Burr Cottage, home to James "Jim" Alexander Hines (1861–1934), upper right, and Bessie Hinson Hines (1882–1966), upper left, who came from Faison, North Carolina, in 1912. Hines ran a gas station and garage with Grover Edwards and Carl Zoellner from 1914 to 1934. He earned his title "Judge Hines" for settling gambling disputes among card players at the tuberculosis sanatorium. (Upper left and lower photographs from Sarah Harkins; upper right photograph from Lewis Dendy.)

John Jay Smith (1853–1941) of
Warren County, Pennsylvania,
came to Highlands from Illinois
in 1878. In 1886, he bought
Arthur House's water sawmill
across Fourth Street from his
own steam sawmill. William
Partridge's gristmill existed
farther downstream. The
two sawmills merged under
Smith's ownership gave him
the advantage of furnishing
most of the building material in
Highlands for the next 30 years.
(Photograph from Earle Young.)

Smith hired Dock McKinney and Joe Henry to run his mill while he served on one occasion as
postmaster and twice as mayor. In the mayoral race, he had the unusual distinction of receiving
every vote cast. He also moonlighted as road surveyor. Between 1904 and 1906, he laid out the
Dillard Road, which for years was known simply as Smith's Road, now Highway 106. (Photograph,
probably by Henry Tanner, from Doris Potts.)

Farmer Wyatt Wiley Smith (1851–1938) from Cornelia, Georgia, married Parthenia Adaline Hedden (1853–1940) of Highlands and built a home in 1878 near Shortoff on 100 acres along the old road to Cashiers Valley and Webster, today's Hicks Road. Wiley, who served the Highlands township as tax collector and deputy sheriff, and Parthenia called their home Spring Oak Lodge when they rented the upstairs bedrooms to travelers and later Sunnyside after their daughter-in-law Edna Smith's favorite song. In 1946, it was home to Col. Fergus Kernan, the World War II military strategist who had written *Defense Will Not Win the War*, the book that prefigured the Normandy invasion of 1944. Later owners of the home discovered a secret upstairs room, which had been boarded up, that they reopened for use as a small bedroom or study. (Photographs from Terry and Al Randall.)

Before 1878, school was held at the log Law House, an early schoolhouse, courthouse, church, and community center. Highlands's first school was built in 1878 by Arthur House at Fourth and Oak Streets. It served students age 6 to 20, ungraded, in a single room from May through August until 1891, when eight grades and six-month terms were established. The Town Clock School replaced it in 1919. (Photograph from the *Highlander.*)

This Highlands School class poses in 1895, the school's last year as Highlands Academy. From left to right are (first row) Ab Edwards, Arthur Griffin, George Cleaveland, Bessie Anderson, Nettie Reese, and twins Helen and Belle McKinney; (second row) Charlie Anderson, Jim Cleaveland, Charlie McKinney, Walter Reese, Will Cleaveland, Jim Munger, Ed Anderson, Georgia Edwards, Tina Anderson, Frank Henry (the teacher's brother), Pearl Brown, Bessie Reese, and teacher Mae Henry. (Photograph from Doris Potts.)

Monroe I. Skinner (1829–1899), a native of Arcade, New York, and Phebe Elizabeth Atwater Skinner (born 1831) built a home in 1878 at Fourth and South Streets that Margaretta Ravenel expanded in 1883 into Islington House (later King's Inn). Skinner had a blacksmith shop at Fourth and Pine Streets and built his second home, Glencroft (pictured above), under Sunset Rock in 1883. Rebecca Harris renamed it Trillium Lodge in 1921. (Photograph from Lewis Dendy.)

Benson W. Wells (1842–1898) and Louise Emmons Wells (1846–1906) built their home at Shortoff in 1878. In 1880, Louise's sister Ella Emmons Hudson (1849–1880), for whom the Hudson Library is named, stayed here and died. Louise's parents, Rev. Henry Ware Emmons (1807–1899) and Elizabeth Whitman Emmons (1818–1899), also died here within three hours of each other, which may be why Annie Pierson swore the house was haunted. (Photograph by the author.)

The first summer residents to settle in Highlands were Samuel Prioleau Ravenel (1822–1902) and Margaretta Amelia Fleming Parker Ravenel (1833–1913) from Charleston. In 1879, they built Highlands's first summer home, called Wantoot after a family plantation near Charleston. At Prioleau's death in 1902, the Ravenels had accumulated 30,000 acres from Highlands to Cashiers Valley, including the primeval forest between Bear Pen and Whiteside Mountains. (Left photograph from Clare Ellis; right photograph from Alison Darby.)

The Ravenel home cost $3,503.50 to construct. Situated at the northern end of Wolf Ridge, it commanded a magnificent view of Horse Cove. On a clear day, the family could sit on their porch and set their clock by the train's arrival in Clemson, South Carolina. Jules Blanc Monroe (1880–1960) and Mabel "May" Overton Logan Monroe (1881–1956) bought the home in 1914, renaming it Playmore. (Photograph from Highlands Historic Inventory.)

Farmer Ebenezer "Eben" Selleck Jr. (1834–1908) and Harriet "Hally" Paley Selleck (born 1834) arrived from Lewisboro, New York, in 1879. A Union army veteran, Selleck left Highlands in early 1881 to serve newly elected Pres. James Garfield as collector of the Port of Philadelphia but returned within a year, after the latter's tragic assassination. He served Highlands twice as major before moving to Seattle in 1905. (Photograph from Taylor's Artillerymen.)

The Sellecks chose the forested Spring Street block between Third and Fourth Streets for their home and barn. When they departed in 1905, ownership transferred to Mrs. Charles Albert Hill (Louise) of Washington, D.C. When the Hills moved to Charleston in 1934, it passed to the family of Lilia Kennard McCall of New Orleans and is affectionately known today as the Rabbit Hole. (Photograph from Highlands Historic Inventory.)

The author of the best history of the region, *Western North Carolina: A History, 1730–1913*, was John Preston Arthur (1851–1916), a native of Columbia, South Carolina. He built a home with his mother and sister in 1879 on Main Street, west of today's Stone Lantern and Cleaveland house. After he moved to New York in 1881, his sister kept the home until 1925. (Photograph from *Western North Carolina*.)

Maj. Joseph Halleck (1822–1899) and Alvina "Vina" Elizabeth McCoy Halleck (1881–1903) of Westernville, New York, built the town's first hotel, Highlands House, in 1880. When John Jay and Mary Chapin Smith owned it in 1886, it was called Smith House, and when Frank Benjamin Cook (1892–1980) and Verna Holbrook Cook (1901–1984) took over in 1925, they renamed it Highlands Inn. (Photograph by John Bundy, August 27, 1883, from Harbison Collection.)

45

When William M. Partridge (1823–1908) from Gustavus, Ohio, arrived in 1880 with Eliza J. Smith Partridge (born 1828), he became the Highlands miller, operating a flour and corn mill downstream from House's sawmill. Around 1900, the Partridges, seeking retirement, invested in a John Ruskin "commonwealth" that failed, leaving them destitute upon their return to Highlands. William never fully recovered, and the town adopted his bereaved widow. (Photograph from Louise Beacham.)

By 1883, the Partridges had built their home on Oak Ridge between Main Street and their gristmill on Mill Creek, which for 20 years ground the common grain for the people of Highlands. After William's death, the family of Luke Rice Sr. occupied the home until Luke's death in 1968. Today it serves the town as its chamber of commerce. (Photograph from Highlands Historic Inventory.)

Jonathan Heacock (1842–1929) of Bucks County, Pennsylvania, and his second wife, Annie Buckley Heacock (1850–1915), came to Highlands from Annie's parents' home in Kansas in 1880. They lived at Dobson's Buttermilk Tract just beyond today's Highlands Country Club. Leaving Highlands to farm grapes in Georgia, they returned in 1891 to live with their 1 ildren in Charles F. Diffenderfer's house at the end of Fifth Street. (Photograph from Richard Melvin.)

The Heacocks (pronounced *Hay-cock*) landscaped their hillside home with native trees and a garden of fruits, berries, and flowers as well as a spring-fed fountain. Heacock crafted furniture and entertained boarders with one of Highlands's first radios, a magic lantern, and his violin, while pursuing his interests in photography and agriculture and reminiscing over the war with fellow Union army veteran and neighbor John Durgin. (Photograph from Highlands Historic Inventory.)

47

Across Horse Cove Road from the home he had built for his father, Mayor Stanhope Hill, Frank Harrison Hill (1856–1949) of Horse Cove built a home for himself in 1880. Here he lived off-and-on for two years while working in Highlands and courting Sarah Frost (1860–1945), the daughter of his new neighbor, Dr. Charles Frost. From 1882 to 1886, this was the home of Franklin "Frank" L. Dimick (1843–1882) and Anna "Annie" G. Dimick (1848–1886), who ran the Cheap Cash Store, Highlands's first chain store. After 1903, the home belonged to the Baltimore publisher pictured above, Nathan Billstein (1859–1931) from Sandusky, Ohio, his wife, Ella Lillian Myers Billstein (1866–1958), and his sister, Dr. Emma Loblein Billstein (1855–1914), before it burned and was rebuilt in 1931. (Upper photographs from Nancy Smith; lower photograph from Don and Carole O'Neal.)

Native Vermonter George A. Cheney (born 1830), a bookkeeper, and Agnes J. Cheney (born 1835) arrived in 1880 from Beloit, Wisconsin, where Cheney ran a bakery. He bought 400 acres of the Mud Ford surrounding today's Cheney Lane, including the shoals of Big Creek, and established a dairy. For raising cattle, a good Jersey or Ayrshire bull (above) was at a premium in Highlands. (Photograph, c. 1890, from Hudson Library Collection.)

For 12 years, from his arrival in the fall of 1880 until his death, the widower Dr. Charles Leonard Frost (1821–1893) from Mosquito Cove, New York, was the town's doctor, residing on Main Street in Hutchinson's vacated house, which he finished building. He married Meta Jane Norton (1864–1942), sold his home to Tudor Tucker Hall, and built Meadow House at the rear of his own property. (Photograph from Luther Turner.)

From 1881 to 1883, year-round residents were arriving from all over the northeast. Henry Martin "H. M." Bascom (1853–1942), a widower and native of Rock Island, Illinois, arrived in 1881 in response to Kesley's pamphlet promoting Highlands as a health resort. He built his home next to Stanhope Hill's house at Sixth and Main Streets. In 1887, he married his apartment tenant Amanda Florence Coffin of Dunreith, Indiana (1858–1943). (Photograph from Bascom Estate.)

Around 1892, Bascom built Chetolah, his second home, on a spur of Satulah Mountain. It included a wood-burning furnace for central heating, something of a rarity at the time. In 1981, this house would sell for an impressive $350,000, much of which contributed to the creation by Watson Barratt (1884–1962) of the Bascom-Louise Gallery, named for Watson's wife, Louise Bascom, and her father. (Photograph from Highlands Historic Inventory.)

In 1883, Bascom built a two-story general merchandise store with a tin roof near the corner of Fourth and Main Streets. Initially a tin shop, it also carried medicine, hardware, sheet metal, and plumbing as well as milk in buckets, meat by the slab, coffee in a barrel, horse collars, plow lines, gumdrops, stick candy, and chewing gum. He also built a large livery stable nearby. (Photograph from Hudson Library Collection.)

In 1889–1990, Bascom built Davis House, a fabulous inn named after his wife's aunt, Mary A. Davis, who managed it. It was known from 1923 to 1935 as Martin House, from 1936 to 1950 as Tricemont Terrace, from 1951 to 1955 as the Bascom-Louise, in 1956 as Kings Inn II, and from 1957 until it burned in 1982 as Lee's Inn, owned and managed by Richard "Dick" and Jean Lee of Orlando, Florida. (Photograph from Hudson Library Collection.)

The editor of Highlands's first newspaper, the *Blue Ridge Enterprise* (1883–1884), was Edwin Evans "E. E." Ewing (1824–1901), a native of the Octoraro hills of Maryland who came with Emma McMurphy Ewing (born 1842) in 1881 from Kansas, having cofounded the *Topeka Capital*, still one of the leading newspapers of the West. The Ewings left for his home in Maryland in 1884. (Photograph from Historical Society of Cecil County, Maryland.)

The Ewings built their home in 1881–1882 on a 40-acre tract, today's site of the Highlands Biological Station and Nature Center on the Horse Cove Road. The house is known today as the J. Manson Valentine house, named for the professor who did the research for Charles Berlitz's book *Bermuda Triangle*. Valentine's wife, Elizabeth, bought the house and had Roy Phillips remodel it in 1945. (Photograph by the author.)

Robert Julius "Jule" Phillips (1857–1915) was a prolific builder. He came from Franklin in 1882 and married James Wright's daughter, Mary Ellen Wright (1853–1929) of Highlands. He built Charles Edwards's first home, Benson Wells's home at Shortoff, and the homes of Dr. W. T. Thompson, H. M. Bascom, Jerry Pierson, and Barak Wright. Phillips also helped build Islington House (King's Inn) and the Presbyterian church. (Photograph from Linda Wright David.)

In 1882, Phillips and Marion Wright bought 141 acres near Short Off Mountain at 12.5¢ an acre, totaling $17.625, and in 1886, Phillips built his home. Initially he had the chimney built in the middle of his home but rebuilt it on the outside wall when one winter night the center stone dropped into the fireplace. The house was torn down in the 1970s. (Photograph, 1925, from Frances Crunkleton Wright.)

Sumner Clark Sr. (1830–1919), from Worcester, Massachusetts, came to Highlands with Ann Mason Clark (1827–1908) in 1882 to become the town's first county superintendent of public instruction. He bought the log Law House and in 1883 built a dry goods and grocery store that became Charlie and Helen Wright's home in 1914, when Sumner left for New Jersey. The home burned in 1929 but was rebuilt. (Photograph from Frances Crunkleton Wright.)

Millwright and machinist Charles A. Boynton (born 1825) from Hollis, New Hampshire, and Rebecca Campbell Boynton (born 1825) built their cottage on Oak Ridge at Third and Main Streets in 1882. After 1905, it became a boardinghouse run by five families, from the Nortons to the Phelps, then Main Street Inn. Boynton built Highlands's first church—Methodist (today's Baptist)—with a lumber mill behind. (Photograph, 1894, from Davene J. Boynton Rusher.)

Charles and Rebecca's two sons, Frank Ellis (1859–1942) and Charles Lawrence "C. L." or "Charlie" (1864–1943), worked at their father's mill on Mill Creek behind today's Mountain High Motel as carpenters, builders, and contractors, but they were also naturalists. Charlie (right) was an expert ornithologist whose specimens and notes established the varieties of many birds in Highlands. Frank (left) made history in the world of botany when, in September 1885, he and Charles Sprague Sargent rediscovered *Shortia galacifolia*, long famous as the extremely rare galax-leaved plant of the *Diapensiaceae* family that was lost for nearly a century after André Michaux had first found it on the southern slopes of the Blue Ridge not far from the Highlands area. (Photograph, 1930, from Susanna Ovel; drawing by Paris Decaisne, 1839.)

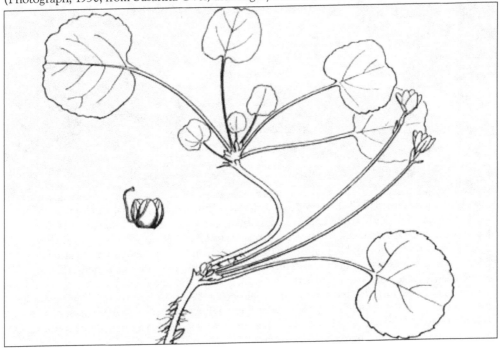

James Elbert Rideout (1838–1907) from Newcastle, New Brunswick, Canada, and Margaret Flavilla Smith Rideout (1843–1912) from Chester, Maine, came to Highlands in 1882. They built a home at Chestnut and Fifth Streets, which they ran as Satulah House for boarders until they could build a new 21-room Satulah House in 1886 farther south on Fifth Street. A Union army veteran, Rideout had a keen sense of humor and intense interest in science and astronomy, having built his own fairly large observatory for the townsfolk to view meteor showers, the moon, and the stars. He predicted in 1898 that Highlands would become "a transient town," that automobiles would travel paved roads with engines powerful enough to climb Satulah Mountain, and that "aeroplanes would fly over Highlands" with mail from Asheville to Atlanta. (Upper photographs from Louise Rideout Beacham; lower photograph by the author.)

The Satulah House that the Rideouts built in 1886 rivaled Highlands House, Islington House, and Central House for comfort and popularity, due in part to Margaret's lively hospitality. Known as "Mother Rideout," she entertained with many parties, including dancing in the dining room. For years after her death in 1912, the house stood abandoned, replaced by the Catholic church in 1950. (Photograph by R. Henry Scadin, 1899, from Special Collections, UNC–Asheville.)

Rideout built his first general store next to Highlands House in 1882 but moved into the long, low Granite Store across Main Street in 1889, soon called the Rock Store. Today it is the first floor of Old Edwards Inn. Characteristic of his brand of humor, he erected signs at the edge of town that read: "Ride in to Rideout's, buy your dry goods, and ride out of town." (Photograph from Doris Potts.)

Alfred Hawkins (1837–1920), a native of Twinsburg, Ohio, purchased 1,000 acres southeast of Highlands for his Rock House Farm in 1883. A farmer by trade but having studied homeopathy, Alfred served the region as doctor, prescribing wild berry, polk sallet, raspberry, and yellowroot cures to alleviate suffering. His wife, Pauline Maria Fuller Hawkins (1843–1929), was equally knowledgeable and independent. She was the daughter of Lois Weisbrooker, the pseudonym for Adeline Eliza Nichols, a prolific 19th-century champion of women's rights—indeed, of women's superiority. Maria was one of the earliest female census takers in North Carolina. Alfred and Maria reared Laura, a teacher and mountain poet; Huber, who traveled with Barnum and Bailey Circus; and Barry, who earned the Thomas Jefferson Award for 60 years of monitoring the area's weather. The whole family was essentially self-educated. (Photographs from Dr. Larry Hawkins.)

Mary Abbie Chapin (1855–1940), a native of Wethersfield, Illinois, arrived in 1883 from Massachusetts. In 1886, she married John Jay Smith and brought to their marriage a most impressive dowry. Her aunt Eliza Wheaton, the founder of Wheaton Seminary (now Wheaton College) in Massachusetts, gave the newlyweds Highlands House, now on the National Register, as a wedding gift. (Photograph from Hudson Library Collection.)

Mary Chapin built Gray Cottage, today's Wolfgang's On Main, which she named for the great botanist Asa Gray, for whom she had painted before coming to Highlands. She created in the woodland setting of Gray Cottage a personal garden that emulated in its exceptional beauty the Anne Hathaway Garden in Stratford, England. She was an accomplished poet and an ardent supporter of the town's library. (Photograph from Highlands Historic Inventory.)

A veteran of the Union army and the Indian Wars, John Henry "Papa" Durgin (1844–1939) from West Rocksbury, Massachusetts, arrived with Martha "Matie" Ann Brown Durgin (1850–1921) in 1883 on a stretcher, prepared to die. Instead, Highlands's healthy climate gave him 56 more years. After the Civil War, Durgin served as personal courier to Gen. George A. Custer from 1866 to 1871 and took part in some of the hardest-fought campaigns against the Cheyennes and Arapahoes, miraculously surviving so many dispatches that he earned the nickname "Reckless Jack" for his courage and daring. One of his four daughters, Bernie, who helped him regain his health in Highlands, would become a nurse for Mary Lapham's tuberculosis sanatorium in 1908, eventually turning her father's property, known as Brookside, into a convalescents' camp after the sanatorium burned in 1918. (Photographs from Carolyn McClanahan.)

In 1883, Monroe Skinner's son, Henry M. Skinner (born 1861), a carpenter, and Mattie O. Skinner (born 1859) built a double store on Main Street with a printing press in the rear and published three Highlands newspapers from 1890 to 1893: the *Star*, *Number Four*, and Thomas Harbison's popular *Mountain Eagle*. This became Hiram Mason Paul's dry goods store from 1897 to 1905, thereafter known as the old Paul store. (Photograph from Hudson Library Collection.)

Highlands's second major physician, after Dr. Frost, was Dr. William "Will" H. Anderson (1840–1912) of Holmes County, Ohio. A veteran of the Union army who believed Highlands to be "the most healthful climate in the world," he arrived in 1883 with his Quaker wife, Susanna "Sudie" Brown Anderson (1852–1940). He bought the 20-acre Webb orchard south of town and established his office in Central House. (Photographs from Elizabeth Rice Harbison.)

61

In 1883, Margaretta Ravenel expanded Monroe Skinner's first home into Islington House, named after an old section of Charleston. It became one of Highlands's most gracious and popular lodgings for summer residents for over a century. In 1925, Robert "Bob" Rutledge King (1874–1950) and Ellie Howard Hudson King (1887–1976) of Anderson, South Carolina, renamed it King's Inn. It burned to the ground in 1994. (Photograph from *King's Inn Cookbook*, 1935.)

Although the Baptists had organized on July 13, 1884, the first church in Highlands to have its own sanctuary was the Methodist Episcopal church, built from 1882 to 1884 by Capt. Charles Boynton. The building was dedicated July 5, 1885, and shared by the Northern and Southern Methodists and the Baptists. When the Methodists moved across Main Street in 1909, they sold their sanctuary to the Baptists. (Photograph from Betty Holt.)

A major landowner in early Highlands was Henry Stewart Sr. (1830–c. 1918) from Hackensack, New Jersey, who came with his first wife, Margaret (born 1832), a Canadian, in 1884. Henry wrote agricultural articles for the *Montreal Star*, *New York Times*, and *American Agriculturalist*. He bought William Dobson's home at First and Main Streets, then moved in 1899 to Fourth and Hickory Streets, which was later Frank Cook's home. (Photograph from Highlands Historic Inventory.)

The First Presbyterian Church was built by Marion Wright and Jule Phillips in 1884–1885 and dedicated September 13, 1885, by James E. Fogartie (1850–1916) from Charleston. Margaretta Ravenel and her sister, Clarissa Burt, funded its construction at a cost of around $3,000. A lovely one-story frame structure, it was placed on the National Register in 1996. (Photograph by R. Henry Scadin, 1897–1898, from Special Collections, UNC–Asheville.)

William Bliss "W. B." Cleaveland (1849–1893) of New York and Ida Estelle "Stell" Bailey Cleaveland (1853–1904) of Rhode Island came from Connecticut in 1884. Initially they occupied Joseph A. McGuire's home on North Fourth Street at today's Recreation Park entrance, but in 1888, they bought the lot next to Annie Dimick's Cheap Cash Store and built the home that still exists next to the Stone Lantern. A mineralogist, Cleaveland had come to Highlands, like many others responding to Samuel Kelsey's promotional brochures, to restore his health but died within 12 years, leaving behind a widow, seven children, and a collection of Native American artifacts valued at $5,000 and nationally known among collectors and ethnologists as one of the most complete in North Carolina. The family home remained with the Cleavelands until Harvey Talley bought it in 1945. (Photographs from W. Arthur Hays Jr.)

Directly across from his home, Cleaveland built his grocery store in 1885. This is where he often traded Native American artifacts for produce. His grocery gave way to Fred Edwards's store in 1920, the site of Ann Jacob's Gallery today. The earliest drawing of Highlands was penned by Cleaveland in 1885 from his first home at the Recreation Park, facing Satulah Mountain. (Photograph from Hudson Library Collection.)

In the spring of 1885, when two bootleggers from Moccasin Township, Georgia, were confined by a U.S. revenuer at Highlands House to await trial, 18 Georgians declared war on Highlands, bivouacking across the street at Central House and laying siege for three days. What followed, when Mayor Henry Bascom declared a state of martial law, constitutes the famous Moccasin War of 1885. (Photograph by George Masa from Beverly Cook Quin.)

A native of Herborn, Germany, Louis Zoellner (1859–1938) immigrated with Margaretta Schafer (1863–1951, holding Willie) to Ohio, where they were married, and then to Highlands in 1884. Zoellner built their home in 1885 at today's Moon Mountain Road, not far from Glen Falls, and set out to raise bees on a small-scale farm. The following year, he joined Prof. Thomas Harbison's newly established Highlands Academy, staffed with 10 teachers offering courses in modern languages, vocal and instrumental music, and drawing and sketching, beyond the normal courses in reading, writing, and arithmetic. He taught German and violin. A former German university professor and a violinist of considerable talent, he was invited back to Germany to play at the coronation of Kaiser Wilhelm II in 1888. (Upper photographs from Ella Mae Zoellner; lower photograph from Highlands Historic Inventory.)

One of Professor Zoellner's contributions to early chamber music in Highlands was his formation of the Highlands String Quartet, composed of himself (second from left) and three members of the Highlands Amateur Orchestra, organized the year before his arrival. The quartet included, from left to right, Frank Stewart Sheldon (1862–1944), architect of Davis House, later Lee's Inn; and two of town founder Samuel Kelsey's sons, Truman (1869–1940) and Harlan (1872–1958), as well as . (Photograph from Doris Potts.)

North Carolinian William W. "Tanner" Cobb (born 1846) and Addie E. Cobb (born 1845) moved from South Carolina to Highlands in late 1885 to set up Highlands Tannery in the spring of 1886. Cobb's newspaper advertisements in the *Highlander* called for "Hides Wanted to Tan on Shares" and "Hides Bought or Taken in Exchange for Leather." He is pictured with his son, Sam. (Photograph by Florence Bascom, 1889, from Hudson Library Collection.)

Union army veteran Theron D. Walden (1838–1906) and Elizabeth Eunice Gribling Walden (1840–1927), both of New York and pictured above, arrived in 1885. They built their home on 11 acres of rocky pasture west of Poplar Street's intersection with Fourth Street. The house was heated by a pot-bellied stove in the sitting room and a cook stove in the kitchen, which Elizabeth fired up daily to cook breakfast and the noon meal. Each morning starting at 5:30, she would milk the cows, feed the chickens, carry water from the spring, bake bread, and maintain a large vegetable garden. She took in boarders for income and had no time for illness. In 1911, Joseph Charles Richert (born 1878) of Alabama and Gertrude Fannie Edwards Richert (1878–1925) of Highlands bought the home, naming it Blackberry Hill. Richert became Highlands's first police chief in 1922. (Photographs from Marvin Moore.)

In 1883, C. L. Martin constructed a building (right) at Fourth and Main Streets to house his Central Meat Market. Here in 1884, Walden set up Highlands's first pharmacy and the first Highlands Bank. But Walden also enjoyed growing cacti and had 350 varieties, the most extensive collection in the South. His son, Frank, worked in his store as a watchmaker and jeweler. (Photograph from Doris Potts.)

Robert "Bob" Walter Reese (1855–1929) came from Franklin in 1885 with Merinda Octavia Womack Reese (1857–1899) to paint the new Presbyterian church, and they loved the village so much they stayed for the rest of their lives. After Merinda's death, Robert married Arie Tallent (1875–1940), pictured. (Left photograph from Allen Reese; right photograph from Dallas Reese Jr.)

New Yorker Henry T. O'Farrell (1824–c. 1906) and Abigail Zubede Loomis O'Farrell (born 1825) came to Horse Cove in 1885 and built their home (shown here) in Highlands at Spruce and Fifth Streets in 1888. A kindhearted, garrulous Irishman, Dr. O'Farrell had a pharmacy from 1887 to 1890 beside Highlands House. R. J. Reynolds visited and personally showed Highlanders how to wrap finely cut tobacco in a thin sheet of paper, calling it a cigarette or "little cigar." Dr. O'Farrell's advertisements touted his "Good Cigars" while advising his customers "not to smoke." In 1894, he drew up the town's first fire ordinance and was mayor for eight terms. He died around 1906, and the house burned in 1938. It was replaced in 1973 by Pinebrook Condominiums, Highlands's first year-round residential apartments. (Upper photographs from Martha Beacham Jackson; lower photograph from Mary Berry.)

In 1886, Prof. Thomas Grant Harbison (1862–1936) walked from Union County, Pennsylvania, to Highlands, North Carolina, and founded Highlands Academy. He taught school until 1896, when he married Jessamine "Jessie" M. Cobb (1868–1954). From 1897 to 1903, he served as collector for Vanderbilt's Biltmore Herbarium and from 1903 to 1933 for Harvard University's Arnold Herbarium. From 1933 until his death, he organized the University of North Carolina's Ashe Herbarium. (Photograph from the Harbison family.)

The Harbisons lived with their children, Gertrude, Dorothea "Dolly," Margaret, and Tom Jr., in the house they bought from town founder Samuel Kelsey in 1893 and at Monroe Skinner's Glencroft until 1921, when they finally built their own home on Walhalla Road (above). Professor Harbison was the first president of the Highlands Scientific Society and was twice mayor of Highlands. (Photograph from Harbison Collection.)

Judson Myron Cobb (1834–1905) and Lucy Dutcher Cobb (1842–1934), both of Vermont, came from Beloit, Wisconsin, in early 1887. Judson's ancestor John Cobb had built America's first iron foundry, and Judson himself was America's first manufacturer of building paper. He and Lucy are buried on private property at a spot surrounded by oak, birch, pine, and balsam trees and covered with rhododendron and trailing arbutus. (Photograph by the author.)

The Cobbs bought and expanded a home that Jackson Johnston had owned around 1869 near today's Highlands Country Club's fifth hole. Legend claims that originally it was a Cherokee log cabin, since Cherokees never lived in teepees. The front door was assembled with wooden pegs, and the walls were made of hand-hewn poplar logs. The Cobbs named their home Altadona ("fine lady"). (Photograph by Henry Scadin, 1895, from Betty Holt.)

Joseph "Joe" Dendy (1865–1945) worked for Henry Bascom from 1887 to 1909, then began planting apple trees at Goldmine. He first married Katie Gibson (1870–1901) and then Dora Peek (1874–1960), above, having six children by each. After World War II, his sons Earl and Clifford started Dendy Orchard, which produced 50 varieties of apples, including Rome beauties, Jonathans, Staymans, McIntoshes, Grimes goldens, red delicious, and golden delicious. (Photograph from Lewis Dendy.)

David Norton (1834–1912), who started Norton Community, and his second wife, Martha "Mattie" Adams Norton (1843–1909), bought Central House in 1888 and managed it until 1905, when they retired to Charles Boynton's home a block away, reputedly because David "preferred the quite outskirts to the bustle of town." Entertaining lavishly at Central House, Mattie had "a joyous spirit that warmed one like a sunbeam." (Photographs from Isabel Chambers.)

Rev. William "Will" Taliaferro Thompson Sr. (1840–1920) from Clarke County, Virginia, and his fourth wife, Agnes "Aggie" Buist Thompson (c. 1875–1930), moved to Highlands from Charleston in 1889. Known as the "Fighting Parson" from his service to the Confederacy, Reverend Thompson renounced war and entered the ministry, becoming a pulpit orator whose eloquence earned him a doctor of divinity degree from Highland University in Kansas. (Photograph from Tommy Thompson.)

The Thompsons built a log home, Clearmont, on Satulah Mountain in 1889. They also created Camp Thompson, called the "Camp," in 1902 on 17 acres around a flat-rock picnic area four miles downstream from Highlands on the Cullasaja River. After Will's death, Aggie married James Lamb Perry Sr., and they expanded their home around the original log cabin. (Photograph from Tommy Thompson.)

Jeremiah "Jerry" Pierson (1850–1912) and Emma Adams Pierson (1853–1925) of Whiteside Cove arrived from Norton Community in 1890. Named after his grandfather, a Cherokee from Jasper County, Georgia, Jeremiah worked as caretaker of the Ravenels' summer home and sold insurance and real estate. His wife's descent from Pres. John Quincy Adams led to naming their first son John Quincy. From left to right are (seated) Emma, Lake (on the step), and Jeremiah; (standing) Porter and Quincy. (Photograph from Dan Reese and Martha Reese Lamb.)

Jeremiah bought Charles Allen's 1878 farmhouse at the base of Satulah Mountain, tore it down, and built the three-story, 24-room Pierson Inn in 1899. For extra rooms, he added two annexes: Piermont (Hemlock) Cottage and Lakemont Cottage. He constructed Highlands's second golf links, designed by George Inglesby, around a lake where Highlands School exists today. In 1993, the inn was demolished. (Photograph from Julie Weaver.)

Confederate veteran Tudor Tucker "T. T." Hall (1844–1918) brought his ailing wife Harriet from Charleston for her health, buying Dr. Frost's home in 1890. After both Harriet and Dr. Frost died in 1893, Tudor married Frost's widow, Meta Norton Frost (1864–1942), above, and by 1900, they had enlarged her home, Meadow House, into a true country manor in Dutch colonial style. Here Meta entertained summer guests, who preferred calling the inn Hall House. The fireplace was set in beautiful Italian marble, and hand-beveled Venetian mirrors hung in the lobby. The Halls converted their pond into a lake and surrounded it with a 10-hole golf course, the 10th being across the lake, which would-be golfers often skipped. Hall House was torn down in 1961. (Upper photographs from Jane Lewis; lower photograph from Doris Potts.)

Farmer John W. Houston (1834–1919) and Juletta "Lette" Malinda Miller Houston (1838–1925) built a home in Shortoff around 1891, but like many residents during the early 1900s, they migrated to Oregon. They sold their home in 1911 to Byers Grant Zachary (1867–1912) and Althea Evitt Zachary (1870–1917) from Cashiers Valley. After 1999, the Zachary family home was replaced by today's soccer field at Zachary Park. (Photograph from Mildred Zachary Wilson.)

Seventh-day Adventists Hiram Mason Paul (1840–1924) from Craftsbury, Vermont, and Francena Willey Paul (1848–1935) came from a potato farm in Limestone, Maine, in 1891. Paul opened a dry goods store in Henry Skinner's building on Main Street. An accomplished carpenter, he bought Heacock's Buttermilk Tract and sawmill off the Dillard Road. In 1905, he moved to Trinity, North Carolina, and entered the furniture business. (Photograph from Arthur Hays Jr.)

Dr. Theodore Lamb (c. 1858–1896) and Jessie Coffin Wotton Lamb (1858–1939) became the first summer residents to live on Satulah Mountain, arriving from Augusta, Georgia, in the fall of 1891. They built Chestnut Lodge, a lovely two-story Queen Anne cruciform house, paneled with clear American chestnut and featuring a cross gable roof, wraparound front porch, circling driveway, pond, and distinctive turnstile gate. (Photograph from Jack A. Wotton.)

Jule Phillips built the Masonic Hall, Blue Ridge Lodge No. 435, at Third and Main Streets in 1892–1893 for $297.85. The Highlands Freemasons were first organized by Thoren Walden. Also home to the Order of the Eastern Star, the building has hosted at various times Highlands's first movies, town hall, Highlands School classes, the Unitarians, the Christian Scientists, a health clinic and dentist office, and public dances. (Photograph from Tommy Chambers.)

A native of Montgomery County, Pennsylvania, the widower John Zeigler Gottwals (1830–1913) arrived from Thomasville, Georgia, in 1892. A retired architect, he built his permanent home in 1896 from timber cut in the Boynton brothers' sawmill on Mill Creek. That year, he married his housekeeper, Martha Norton (1854–1944), 23 years his junior. They both supervised construction of the current Methodist church when it relocated in 1909. (Photograph from Tammy Lowe.)

Gottwals designed the outside weather-boarded walls of his home to protrude from many different angles so as to withstand strong winds. Even the main rooms had unusual shapes, several with eight walls of chestnut sheathing. The doorbell was a trigger atop an ornate doorknob. A third-floor turret chamber, sheathed on the exterior with fish-scale shingles, served as the "pouting room," offering peace and solitude for reading. (Photograph from Highlands Historic Inventory.)

Perhaps the most famous of Highlands's physicians was Dr. Mary E. Lapham (1860–1936), above left, a Michigan banker's daughter destined for banking who visited Highlands in 1893, noticed the need for medical care, and changed her profession. She bought a home on Satulah in 1897, which she named Faraway, and in 1908 established one of the first—if not the first—sanatoriums in North Carolina for the cure of tuberculosis. Located on the site of today's Recreation Park, it was known locally as the San or Bug Hill. In 1918, when Bug Hill burned and Dr. Lapham joined the Red Cross during the Great War, nurse Bernie Durgin (1874–1941), above right, moved 25 cottages to Chestnut Street to continue the cure. One of these cottages is preserved at Highlands Historic Village. (Upper left and bottom photographs from the Tom Crumpler Collection; upper right photograph from Carolyn McClanahan.)

Nationally recognized as a pioneer in the field of the artificial pneumothorax treatment of tuberculosis (involving the artificial collapse of one lung to give it rest), Dr. Lapham prescribed lots of fresh air for her patients. She had 60 open-air cottages constructed with wooden sides and floors and canvas-lined roofs that allowed tubercular patients to sleep exposed to the crisp, clear mountain air and sunshine. (Photograph from Tom Crumpler Collection.)

William Calvin "Cal" Speed Jr. (1864–1937) of Rabun County, Georgia, and Alpha Angeline Carver Speed (1862–1941) settled on 100 acres in Shortoff in 1893. Cal trapped his own deer hides, which he hand-tanned and sewed into buckskin shoes, fastening the soles with hand-carved, soft maple pegs. A self-sufficient man, he also produced his own tools. Cal was rarely seen without his mule, Little Jack. (Photograph from Betty Speed Wood.)

If there are more Potts than pans in Highlands, it's due to William T. "Billy" Potts (1857–1935) and Martha "Mattie" Jane Ammons Potts (1862–1929) from Cullasaja. Billy ran a livery between Franklin and Highlands in 1894 before building a stable on Main Street in 1902. Mattie managed Central House from 1905 to 1914. In 1926, sons Frank and Roy Potts replaced the stable with Potts Brothers groceries. (Photograph from Jessie Potts Owens.)

The cottage of Martha Alden Crosby (1841–1940) of Bangor, Maine, and her daughter Mary "May" Josephine Crosby (born 1872) had three stories and, according to the *Galax News*, "heaven knows how many rooms" at the corner of Fifth and Spruce Streets. The Crosby family arrived from San Mateo, Florida, in 1896, and still owns the home. (Photograph from Highlands Historic Inventory.)

After 17 years of services in Highlands without a sanctuary, today's Episcopal Church of the Incarnation was consecrated on August 19, 1896, by circuit rider Rev. John Archibald Deal (1844–1928). Built by Will and Joe McGuire of Franklin at a cost of just over $2,000, the church's high-pitched roof and circular belfry crowned with beauty the strength of its sturdy chestnut and tulip-poplar timbers. (Photograph from Tom Crumpler.)

Carpenter William "Bill" Peary Wilson (1866–1947) and Rebecca "Becky" Speed Wilson (1867–1932) came from Rabun County, Georgia, around 1896–1897, living for two years in Horse Cove and then in Highlands. Bill was a democrat and admired Pres. Woodrow Wilson so much he named a son after him. His son Barnett "Barney" Wilson and Barney's sons were known for their plumbing, heating, and sheet-metal work. (Photographs from Louis "Dud" Wilson.)

The first to settle Laurel Heights, which later became Webbmont, were Thomas "Tom" Brownlow Crunkleton (1871–1948) and Lydia Octavia "Octa" Rogers Crunkleton (1872–1951), shown here. They brought Tom's parents, Joseph Wellington "J. W." Crunkleton (1835–1900) and Sarah Ann Keener Crunkleton (1837–1923) with them from Rabun County, Georgia, in 1897. This was when "painters" (panthers) roamed the plateau and entered their kitchen through the curtain over the door. (Photograph from Walter Taylor.)

Confederate army surgeon and professor at the University of the South and Tulane University Dr. John Barnwell Elliott (1841–1921) of Savannah and Harriott Lucas "Lucy" Huger Elliott (1847–1931) of Charleston built their home on Satulah around 1900. Their son, architect Huger (pronounced *U-gee*) Elliott, designed the Hudson Library, where their daughters, Lucy and Charlotte, became librarians. Charlotte founded the Highlands League of Women Voters in 1923. (Photograph from Highlands Historic Inventory.)

Four

1900–1930

After the turn of the 20th century, Highlands had a Mediterranean showplace known as Cheeononda Garden at the Sloan Estate on Satulah Mountain. Consisting of seven hillside terraces supported by dry walls of native stone—some crowned with carved balustrades, classical urns, and statuary—it featured natural flora of the mountainside, including rhododendron, laurel, and native trees but also Italian imports. (Photograph by George Masa from the Sloan Estate.)

Cheeononda (meaning in Cherokee "little hills upon little hills") has been documented, photographed, and dated from 1901 to 1979 by the Smithsonian Institution. It was the creation of Philadelphia native Henry Worrell Sloan (1861–1944), a New Orleans cotton broker, who came in 1900. He first married Katherine Depew (1860–1928) and later Daisy Moody (1878–1941), who are buried on either side of him on a lower terrace of the garden. (Photograph from the Sloan Estate.)

Sloan's Italian-style house still crowns the garden. He owned one of the first cars in Highlands, but his first wife, Katherine, refused to ride in it, so he had to keep the horse-drawn carriage and a coachman for her. It was Sloan who brought the first movies to Highlands, silent films shown in the school auditorium from 1920 until talkies appeared in 1932. (Photograph from the Sloan Estate.)

Highfield was the second summer home built on Satulah. A three-story house on a promontory of the lower slope, its semicircular living room and wraparound verandah embraced splendid views of Whiteside and Bear Pen Mountains. It was reached from the Walhalla Road by a rustic gate opening into a rhododendron tunnel winding its way along a flag-stoned path up to the piazza. The house was named after the English family home of Florence Charlotte Davies Cropp Perry (1860–1942), above right, who arrived from Charleston with Wade Hampton Perry (1852–1919), above, of Dorchester, South Carolina, in 1900 and started the tradition of welcoming all to their porch for socializing and a refreshing respite from the hot Southern summers. Their daughter, Florence "Flo" Perry Saussy (1896–1976), and George Stone Saussy (1898–1964) continued the tradition. (Photographs from Suzanne Foley Jackson.)

In 1901, Augustus Caesar "A. C." or "Gus" Holt (1878–1964) of Franklin married Judson Cobb's daughter, Gertrude Cobb (1872–1960), and moved to Oregon but returned to Highlands in 1905, buying and farming Hiram Paul's Buttermilk Tract on the Dillard Road. In 1927, he set up a soda fountain at Fourth and Main Streets in the store where Thoren Walden had had his drugstore. He served sandwiches and carbonated soda water, stocked magazines and souvenirs, and even provided curb service with trays for personal delivery to cars parked outside. He was aided by his sons, Bill, Harry, and Lawrence, until 1939, when Bill took over Bill's Soda Shop (1939–1972), Harry established Harry's Café next door, and Lawrence set up a mirror shop. (Photographs from Betty Holt.)

Robert "Bob" Brockbank Eskrigge (1868–1945), a native of New Brighton, England, and one of the South's foremost cotton buyers for English firms, came from New Orleans with Virginia King Logan Eskrigge (1877–1953) in 1907 to begin building their home, World's End, near the southern cliffs of Satulah. Originally intending a log house, they had stones, which were readily available from the mountain, quarried instead and transported on sleds. A Craftsman-inspired Tudor cottage designed by Sam Labouisse, World's End was built from 1908 to 1911 from clear chestnut, hemlock, and birch with oak flooring, the gray-stone walls laid in the English style by skilled Italian and local masons. Equipped for gas lamps, the house was also wired for electricity long before Highlands had electrical power. A furnace in the cellar burned 6-foot logs for central heating. (Upper photograph from Tatham Hertzberg; lower photograph from Bascom Collection.)

Levi Butler Crane (1867–1939) and his second wife, Lucinda Jane "Janie" Morgan Crane (1877–1935), arrived first in 1906 from Pine Mountain, Georgia, settling permanently around 1911. In 1917, they built a stable on Main Street across from today's Methodist church, and Levi and son Phil ran a freight line hauling produce and building materials between Dillard and Highlands. (Photograph from Lassie Crane Buchanan.)

In 1926, they built their home on Oak Street and a barn that Levi and son Frank Crane (1906–1974) replaced with Crane's Riding Stable in 1964. For the next 30 years, rides for young and old alike were extremely popular—guided by Chester, Oscar, Kathy, Carlton, and Clarence and priced at $1 to $2 an hour—until discontinued in 1996. (Photograph from Highlands Historic Inventory.)

In addition to the stable on Main Street and the Oak Street barn, there was a stable at Chestnut and Fifth Streets for rides up Big and Little Bear Pen Mountains, out the Bowery Road, or on the Kelsey Trail to Whiteside; another near the caretaker's house at Highlands Estates for rides to Glen Falls; and one at Helen's Barn for climbing Satulah (pictured). (Photograph by George Masa from Beverly Cook Quin.)

Minnie Doran Warren (1867–1954) of Stockton, New York, bought Kelsey's home from Professor Harbison when she arrived in 1909, naming it Kanonah. In 1918, she had Walter Reese and Leon "Deadeye" Potts build her a home, which became the Hedges, on Satulah. Minnie generously paid off a mortgage when someone was in need and bought cows as gifts for large families. (Photograph from Highlands Historic Inventory.)

Dr. Alexander "Alex" Pierce Anderson (1862–1943) and Lydia McDougal Johnson Anderson (1876–1934) came from Minnesota in 1906. Their home, built by Roy Phillips from 1906 to 1909 in the Scottish tradition for Anderson's Scottish wife, had a barn, an icehouse, sheds, and a clay tennis court. Unique for the times, it employed a windmill to pump water from a well to the kitchen and second-floor bathrooms. Except for its cypress doors, it was made entirely of native wood—maple, white pine, hemlock, oak, poplar, and cherry—and was insulated with mineral wool, similar to today's rock wool. Total cost was $13,770. From 1926 to 1962, this home was owned by William "Will" Woodward Sullivan (1874–1937) and Anne Allender Patrick Sullivan (1876–1963) of Anderson, South Carolina. It was dismantled in 1973 and replaced by Carolina Square. (Upper photographs from *Alexander P. Anderson: 1862–1943* (Hedin, et al.); lower photograph from Highlands Historic Inventory.)

Dr. Anderson was the inventor of the popular Quaker Puffed Wheat and Rice breakfast cereals. Based on Dr. Heinrich Meyer's theory that starch granules contain a miniscule amount of condensed water, Anderson's first experiment in 1901 involved heating corn starch in sealed test tubes to 500 degrees Fahrenheit and then causing it to explode so that the condensed water, flashing into steam, turned each granule into a porous expanded mass. From 1901 to 1941, the Anderson Puffed Rice Company was a wholly owned subsidiary of the Quaker Oats Company of Chicago. By 1905, puffed rice and wheat were being packaged and advertised as foods muzzle-loaded into retort "cannons of murderous caliber that would have been in place on a colonial frigate" and, in simplified terms, "Shot from Guns." (Photographs from Anderson biography.)

He Invented the Foods

Shot from Guns

You owe these puffed foods, and all your delight in them, to Prof. A. P. Anderson.

He was seeking a way to break up starch granules so the digestive juices could get to them.

He was aiming to blast the starch granules to pieces by an explosion of steam.

When he did this, he found that he had created the most enticing cereal foods in existence.

Note the curious process

The whole wheat or rice kernels are put into sealed guns. Then these guns are revolved, for forty minutes, in a heat of 550 degrees.

This terrific heat turns the moisture in the grain to steam, and the pressure becomes tremendous.

Then the guns are fired. Instantly the steam explodes every granule into myriads of particles.

The kernel of grain is expanded eight times. It becomes four times as porous as bread.

Yet the wheat or rice berry remains shaped as before. We have simply the magnified grain.

Puffed Wheat, 10c — Puffed Rice, 15c

There was never a cereal food half so delicious. Never one more digestible.

Think of unbroken wheat or rice berries puffed to eight times their size.

They are so porous that they melt in the mouth. Yet they are crisp.

Let the Children Know

Get one package of the Quaker Puffed Rice, and one of the Quaker Puffed Wheat.

Get both, because they differ vastly. Let the children decide what they want.

Don't wait till tomorrow — order them now. For you are missing a food that's better than any you know.

Exact Size of Grains After Being Puffed

Only one African American is listed in the 1880 census, 28 in 1900, and 8 in 1910. These African Americans were family servants, hotel employees, day laborers, mail carriers, or laundresses and usually boarded or rented. Day laborer Henry Brown (born 1860) and laundress Addie McDaniel Brown (born 1855), however, owned their home at Third and Spring Streets. Addie is shown with Stell (left), Nellie, and George Cleveland in 1900. (Photograph by Henry Scadin from Arthur Hays Jr.)

The other African Americans who owned a home in early Highlands were Mack McAfee (born 1870), a teamster at the sanatorium, and Mary McAfee (born 1870). In 1910, they paid Henry Bascom $350 for a wooden-shingled frame house on Laurel Street, today's Fibber McGee's Closet. In 1916, the Hudson Library authorized them "by the white light of reason" to borrow books. They departed Highlands in 1923. (Photograph from Highlands Historic Inventory.)

The second oldest library in North Carolina, created in 1880 by Louise Emmons Wells from a single box of books as a memorial to her sister, Ella Emmons Hudson, was served for almost 50 years (1926–1975) by Professor Harbison's dedicated daughters: librarian Gertrude Harbison (1903–1980) and her assistant, Dorothea "Dolly" Harbison (1905–1999). They would regularly walk the 5 miles round-trip from their home south of Satulah. (Photograph from Harbison Collection.)

Although originally housed in Highlands's first school, the Hudson Library moved in 1915 when architect Huger Elliott designed and Walter Reese built its new home on Main Street next to the Episcopal church. It served the town until 1985, when a larger Hudson Library replaced it. In 2002, the old building was moved to Fourth Street to become the Highlands Historical Society's Museum and Archives. (Photograph from Hudson Library.)

Certainly the most famous tale of near-tragedy in Highlands history is the incredible heroism of Charles "Charlie" N. Wright (1873–1927) at Whiteside Mountain, above. On May 14, 1911, a group of young picnickers were enjoying a Sunday outing. Gus Baty, age 26, slipped off Fool's Rock and fell 60 feet to the brink of the mountain's 1,800-foot vertical cliff. For his incredible courage in rescuing Gus, Charlie, age 38, received one of only 19 gold medals ever awarded by the Carnegie Commission. The rescue, aided by Will Dillard, took two and a half hours. With the award money, Charlie bought Sumner Clark's home and land, where in 1932 his wife (above), Helen "Oopie" Pauline Cabe Wright (later Wilson) (1892–1959), would build Helen's Barn, famous until 1984 as a mecca for square dancers and buck dancers. (Upper photographs from Frances Crunkleton Wright; bottom photograph from *Land of the Sky*.)

Initially the Carnegie Commission in Pittsburgh hesitated to award Charlie the gold medal, for gold was restricted solely to cases where every requirement was met. But when Rev. G. W. Belk (pictured here on Fool's Rock) led the skeptical investigator to the edge of Whiteside Mountain and down to Fool's Rock, he took one look and, "shaking like an aspen leaf," ended his report. Charlie had earned the gold. (Photograph from Linda Wright David.)

Frances Wright called Helen's Barn "the great equalizer," for it amalgamated everyone in town, winter and summer residents alike, into a single class. Square dancing remained so popular during the summer season that it filled four nights a week. Among the musicians were Donald, Dixie, Mel, and Shirley Keener; Ollie Mae Burrell; Bobby Abbott; Corbin Ledford; Hattie and Pratt McClure; Wally Henry; and Johnny Talley. (Photograph from Maxie Wright Duke.)

Widower William Smith "W. S." Davis (1864–1955) from Hampton, Georgia, came to Highlands in 1914 seeking a cure at Dr. Lapham's sanatorium. He married Jeremiah Pierson's daughter, Rebecca Lake Pierson (1878–1960), and set up a grocery store in Jeremiah's Rock Store, which always smelled of brown sugar, shoe leather, and cheese. He served five terms as mayor. (Left photograph from Edith Nix; right photograph from Dan Reese and Martha Reese Lamb.)

When Rebecca Smallwood Harris (1869–1960) of Havana, Cuba, arrived with her brother, Isaac Leonard Harris (born 1861), from Florida in 1918, they built a home at Gibson and Horse Cove Roads but in 1921 moved to Monroe Skinner's Glencroft. Renaming it Trillium Lodge, Rebecca retained the 50 acres until her death in 1960, when it was subdivided as Sunset Hills around Harris Lake. (Left photograph from Marie Edwards; right photograph from Julie Gary.)

Fredrick "Fred" Alexander Edwards (1896–1954) and Canty Picklesimer Edwards (1902–1963), above, came to Highlands from Horse Cove in 1916. Edwards replaced Cleaveland's old grocery, owned by Charlie Wright, with a new building. For over 30 years, from 1920 to 1952, the Fred Edwards Store (right) offered staple and fancy groceries, notions, dry goods, and friendly, gracious service. In winter, old-timers stood with their backs to the big potbellied stove, warming themselves and exchanging stories while they passed the time of day, two or three hound dogs asleep at their feet. Next to Fred Edwards's store was the equally popular Potts Brothers grocery (1926–1956), run by W. T. Potts's sons Frank Huffman Potts (1888–1960) and William Roy "Nick" Potts (1892–1964). In 1952, Frank's son, John Stephen "Steve" Potts, converted Fred Edwards's store into Steve's Country Store. (Upper photographs from Fredricka Langford; bottom photograph from Betty Holt.)

Charles "Charlie" Junior Anderson (1898–1962) came from Westminster, South Carolina, in 1921, married Mattie Angela Hall (1898–1982), and around 1925 built a drugstore, 5¢-and-10¢ variety store, and Texaco station next to his home on Fourth Street Hill (shown here in 1938). During the 1930s, this was a popular gathering place for residents entertained by Amos and Andy at their peak of radio fame. During the 1950s, it was where the bus stopped for travelers to Atlanta, Chattanooga, Knoxville, Asheville, Charlotte, Columbia, and Augusta. The five-and-dime store was filled with fascinating, affordable items displayed in wooden cubbies on countertops and spinner racks, offering everything from hairpins and nail polish to popguns and children's dress-up high heels. (Upper photographs from Jane Lewis; lower photograph from Hudson Library Collection.)

Brothers George W. Marett (second syllable accented) (1873–1963) and Stephen Thompson "S. T." Marett (first syllable accented) (1862–1943) arrived with their wives, Jessie George Marett (1876–1958) and Leila Coanza Lewis Marett (1867–1954), from Fair Play, South Carolina, in 1922. S. T. directed Highlands Bank (1923–1933) on Fourth Street Hill with the philosophy, "It isn't what you make that counts. It's what you save." George is shown at right. (Photograph from Tammy Lowe.)

In 1925, George Marett bought Bascom's store at Main and Fourth Streets and had Will Cleaveland double its size to add a grocery while renaming Bascom's store Highlands Hardware. The hardware store lasted only five years before moving to Fourth Street Hill and then to east Main Street. Above the grocery was Agnes Medlock's and Pearl Walker's Highlands Tea Room, one of the first to thrive in Highlands. (Photograph from Hudson Library Collection.)

Col. John S. Sewell (1869–1940) and Agnes Lyon Sewell (1864–1954) came from Birmingham, Alabama, in 1926. A retired U.S. Army engineer, Sewell designed some of the most notable public buildings in the nation's capital: the Government Printing Office, Department of Agriculture, Army War College and Engineers' School, and U.S. Soldiers' Home. He was recognized by the American Society of Civil Engineers for his design of reinforced concrete for fire-resisting structures. In 1917, he commanded the 17th Railway Construction Regiment at St. Nazaire, France, supervising 39,000 troops and millions of tons of shipped material. Between his birth in a simple log cabin in Tennessee and his death in this log cabin (photographed by George Masa) in Highlands, he led a life of complex and elegant design. (Upper photographs from Frances Crunkleton Wright; bottom photograph from Beverly Cook Quin.)

Joseph Edwin Root (1881–1967) of Lincoln, Nebraska, and Addie Cottingham Ridgely Root (1877–1961) of Charleston, South Carolina, arrived in 1925, and for the next 30 years, their home, which they built at Main and Third Streets, became Addie's popular gift shop and tearoom. Joseph was hired in 1928 as a construction engineer for the new Highlands Estates Golf Course. Reeves Hardware replaced their home in 1967. (Photographs from Mary Elizabeth Cone.)

The founder and first president of the Highlands Biological Station in 1927 was Clark Howell Foreman (1902–1977) from Atlanta. In founding the station, Clark argued, "I do not know of a town that can claim relatively so much intellectual history as that possessed by Highlands. From the first, people have been attracted to it by the beauty and grandeur of the natural environment." (Photograph from Highlands Biological Station.)

The town butcher was Nettie Rice's son, Luther "Luke" Warren Rice (1881–1968), who married Dr. Will Anderson's daughter, Christina Sarah Anderson (1885–1925), and lived in William Partridge's home, today's chamber of commerce, from 1909 to 1968. Luke sold native beef and lamb in the back of W. S. Davis's Rock Store until he had his own building in 1928 at the site of today's Wit's End, between the 1940–1966 post office and Potts Brothers grocery. Luke's shepherd dogs, Bill and Jack, herded sheep, cattle, and hogs to the slaughter long before the age of trucks. Luke served 34 years on the town council and was town clerk when Highlands acquired water and electric systems at the end of the 1920s. Christina was a poet and Hudson librarian shortly before her death at age 40. (Upper left photograph from Tammy Lowe; upper right photograph from W. Herbert Rice; bottom photograph from Betty Holt.)

Among Highlands's greatest benefactors have been the Woodruffs. George Waldo Woodruff (1895–1987) and Irene Tift King Woodruff (1898–1982) began coming to Highlands in 1928. They built Ruffwood in 1939. From 1936 to 1985, George was a director of the Coca-Cola Company, which his father had bought from Asa Chandler's family for $25 million in 1919. George and his daughter Jane funded the creation of the much-needed Highlands Civic Center at the former site of Dr. Lapham's sanatorium as a memorial to Woodruff's late wife just before his own death in 1985. In 2004, Jane Woodruff funded a medical building and a clinic for the Highlands-Cashiers Hospital. The Woodruffs have made extraordinary contributions to education, recreation, and medicine both in Georgia and in North Carolina. (Portraits by Prudence Carter Fuller in 1991 and 1995; photograph from Highlands Historic Inventory.)

Highlands's first country club golf course, designed by Donald Ross, was built in the highest range east of the Rockies to challenge even the fancy shooting of golf-legend Robert "Bobby" Tyre Jones Jr. (1902–1971). In 1929, Jones christened the just-completed first nine holes by playing twice, with a triumphant 69, beating the much-ballyhooed par of 70 on his first try. (Photograph from Sidney Matthew's *Life and Times of Bobby Jones*.)

During the summer of 1930, the Highlands course became a practice ground for Jones. He so improved his accuracy that by year's end he had accomplished a feat never before—or since—equaled, winning all four amateur and open championships in Great Britain and the United States in the same year: the Grand Slam. Linton H. Young designed Jones's home on Little Yellow Mountain. (Photograph from Highlands Historic Inventory.)

Five

ARCHITECTURAL GEMS

Early Highlands homes and stores were erected by pioneer builders Jule Phillips, Frank Hill, John Jay Smith, Marion Wright, Charles Boynton, and Boynton's sons Frank and Charlie. The creator of a jewel of early Highlands, however, remains unknown: the architect/builder of the Town Clock School, 1916–1919. With its four-faced clock and 360-pound bell, it was the imperial crown of the town until its demise in 1960. (Photograph from Allen Reese.)

The builder of the old jailhouse on Maple Street (1917–1918), which replaced the 1885 calaboose at Fourth and Pine Streets, was W. B. Cleaveland's son William Monroe "W. M." or "Will" Cleaveland (1886–1932). It was Will who, with Quincy Pierson, co-drafted the town's first building codes in 1919. His planing and blacksmith shop stood on North Fourth Street beside Mill Creek until 1941. (Photograph from Georgia Cleaveland Sanders.)

Cleaveland built Harbison's home in 1920–1921, six loafer's benches on Main Street in 1922, Highlands Bank on Fourth Street Hill in 1923, Anderson's drug and dime stores in 1924–1925, the two-story addition and dormers for Central House in 1925, Marett's Main Street grocery in 1925, the first clubhouse at Highlands Estates (pictured) in 1928–1930, and Weyman Laboratory for the biological station in 1930. (Photograph from Highlands Country Club.)

Robert Reese's son, Joseph Walter Reese Sr. (1881–1960), demanded perfection in any work he supervised. In overseeing construction of the post office, he found that the first floorboard was laid "so crooked that a black snake could hardly run it." He made the workers rip the floor up and nail it down straight, claiming it had to be "pig tight and bull strong." (Photograph from Allen Reese.)

Reese built the homes of Dr. William Weston, Craig Cranston, Henry Sloan, Sloan's sister-in-law Alice Depew Lyons (pictured), Minnie Warren, and Edward Moore on Satulah, as well as his own home next to Dusty Rhodes Superette on the Dillard Road, the two-story brick-and-tile post office (1940–1966) next to Wit's End on Main Street, and scores of other homes in Highlands. (Photograph by George Masa from Beverly Cook Quin.)

Hiram Paul's son Guy Paul Sr. (1885–1952) was a blacksmith, brick mason, carpenter, logger, machinist, miller, and construction foreman. He helped build Lake Sequoyah Dam in 1926 and from 1927 to 1929 the scenic Franklin Road, which was literally carved into the sheer rock walls of the Cullasaja River Gorge, falling with the river almost 2,000 feet in only seven or eight miles. (Photograph from Jessie Potts Owens.)

Paul helped build the first Highlands Estates clubhouse and dam from 1928 to 1930. He built his own home, subsequently known as Pippin's Roost, around 1930 and rebuilt Highlands Baptist Church in 1940. Even to this day, the acoustics in the wood-shingled high school auditorium, which he built in 1934 and which still serves as the Highlands Playhouse, are nearly perfect. (Photograph from Highlands Historic Inventory.)

Jule Phillips's son, James Roy Phillips (1889–1945), built Alexander P. Anderson's mansion in the Pine Street block between Fourth and Fifth Streets from 1906 to 1909 and Robert B. Eskrigge's World's End on Satulah from 1908 to 1911. He helped Guy Paul build Lake Sequoyah Dam in 1926 and constructed 21 homes from 1931 to 1942. Many were designed by architects Richard L. Aeck, Linton H. Young, and Louis A. Edwards. (Photograph from Linda Wright David.)

Among Phillips's homes were those of Mrs. Clark Howell and E. F. Raynor at Highlands Country Club; Lilla Nourse and Mary Hanckel on Bear Pen Mountain; Mrs. Bailey Maddox on Little Yellow Mountain; George Townsend, Charles Holcomb, and Arthur Bliss (pictured) near Whiteside Mountain; Gen. Colden Ruggles on Whiteside; Mrs. Kenyon Zahner on Billy Cabin; and Mrs. Shephard on Mirror Lake. (Photograph from Edna Phillips Bryson.)

Billy Webb's grandson Joe Webb (1881–1950), often aided by his stepson Furman Vinson, built 36 houses from 1922 to 1938, most of which featured his now-famous rustic log-cabin style and two of which are on the National Register. Joe lived in Tom Crunkleton's first home in Laurel Heights, where he built 13 homes and in 1931 was declared mayor of Webbmont, as the area is now called. (Photograph from Danette Webb.)

Webb built log homes on Bear Pen, Billy Cabin, Satulah, and Cullasaja Drive and on all roads leading into and out of Highlands. He built the Kenyon Zahner summer home (shown here) and boathouse on Lake Sequoyah, which burned in 1971, and today's restaurant On the Verandah, originally the Dugout, a roadside tavern that thrived for 24 years on wine, beer, and square dancing. (Photograph from Bob Zahner.)

Six

ARTISTIC CREATIONS

Highlands is well known as an artist's haven for the quality and variety of art produced. Among early works that focused on local scenes were the landscape tableaux of John Jay Smith and Jennie M. Burlingame (born 1886), created in 1929 from mosses, lichens, ferns, bark, hornet's nests, and delicately tinted bits of cotton, actually more natural than oil paintings of the same scenes. (*Bridal Veil Falls* from Mary Cumming Fitzhugh.)

Highlands's first photographer was John Elwood Bundy (1853–1933) from Greensboro, North Carolina, whose Quaker family moved when he was five to Indiana. There, primarily self-taught but encouraged in art by James Whitcomb Riley, Bundy painted portraits and panoramic pastoral and woodland scenes that reflected his profound love of nature and earned him the distinctive title "Dean of the Richmond Group" of landscape artists. (Photograph © Richmond Art Museum, Richmond, Indiana.)

Bundy was a photographer before he chose in 1896 to devote himself exclusively to painting. It was his love of the Blue Ridge Mountain scenery that he credited as "marking out the path I have followed," and in 1883, he came to Highlands to photograph street scenes (such as this of Main Street) and views of the mountains and waterfalls to exhibit at Bascom's store. (Photograph by John Bundy from Doris Potts.)

Michigan native R. Henry Scadin (1861–1923), pictured here at Glen Falls, came to North Carolina around 1889. He photographed the local scenery and people near the present towns of Brevard, Tryon, Saluda, Sapphire, and Asheville, extending as far west as Highlands. The University of North Carolina at Asheville has over 1,200 of his glass negatives dating from 1889 to 1920 and his diaries. (Photograph by Wesley Clifford from Harbison Collection.)

Scadin photographed Highlands during 16 years, from 1896 to 1912, but mostly in 1897–1898 and 1910. For perspective and composition as well as graphic detail, he captured extraordinary sights of mountains, cliffs, forests, and waterfalls; inns, churches, and businesses; residents and their homes; and country roads. He sold his photographs, such as this c. 1908 image of Highlands, through Baxter White, H. M. Bascom, Alex Anderson, Frank Walden, and Capt. Prioleau Ravenel. (Photograph from Hudson Library Collection.)

Pittsburgh-native Henry Ossawa Tanner (1859–1937), an African American artist and photographer verging on bankruptcy and depression in Atlanta, came to Highlands during the summer of 1889, and his hard times, as he marveled, "vanished as the mountain mists before the sun." Inspired by Highlands's natural setting to rededicate himself to art, he moved to Paris and became one of the most distinguished American realists of the early 20th century. (Photograph from Smithsonian Archives of American Art.)

Among Tanner's landscape, genre, and Biblical works, the most famous are his *Banjo Lesson* (1893) and *The Thankful Poor* (1894), with their focus on African American pride and dignity. The painting that best represents Tanner's stay in Highlands is his *Mountain Landscape, Highlands, North Carolina* (1889), which hangs in the art department of Berea College, Kentucky, and shows Whiteside Mountain and Black Rock from Satulah Mountain. (Photograph from Berea College Collection.)

Variously known as the Japanese Ansel Adams and "the greatest photographer of the Great Smoky Mountains," George Masa (c. 1881–1933), born as Masahara Izuka, came to America in 1901 and to North Carolina in 1915. In 1929, Frank Cook hired him to photograph the Highlands environs, resulting in nearly 100 large-format shots of local homes, street scenes, and falls, including impressive views of Whiteside Mountain. (Photograph from Bonesteel Films.)

Perfectionist that he was, Masa stayed in Highlands for two weeks, often refusing to take a picture unless the light was exactly right. Some of his most impressive shots are of Dry Falls, Bridal Veil Falls, the Cullasaja River Gorge road under construction, the primeval forest, Satulah cliffs, the Sloan gardens, homes of summer residents, and mountain vistas, such as his Whiteside from Satulah. (Photograph from Beverly Cook Quin.)

Savannah native Rosine Raoul (1885–1918) was one of the few unfortunates who moved to Highlands in 1915 to benefit from Dr. Lapham's cure of tuberculosis, which was killing one American every 15 seconds, but lost her fight for life in 1918. At her death, she was an actress, poet, playwright, essayist, and illustrator, having attended Pratt Institute and Veltin School in New York City. (Photograph from Emory University Rare Book Library.)

Raoul's journals, letters, poems, sketchbooks, and book illustrations are archived at Emory University Library, including writings by her sister, Eléonore Raoul Greene (1888–1983), onetime owner of Brushy Face Mountain, one of the South's earliest advocates of women's rights, and Emory Law School's first female graduate. Rosine too was an early suffragette. Her 1900 drawing of *Great Hill Place*, her grandmother's home in Bolingbroke, Georgia, is below. (Drawing from Margaret Rhodes Shaffner.)

George Bagby Matthews (1857–1944) painted oil portraits of American historical figures, such as Patrick Henry and John Paul Jones, while he was restoring artwork in the U.S. Capitol from 1928–1935. He also painted Confederate heroes like Jefferson Davis, Stonewall Jackson, Lee and his generals, and scenes such as *Battle of the Merrimac with the Monitor* and *Last of the Wooden Navy*. (Portrait from the Virginia Historical Society.)

In 1931, while visiting his friend Dr. Percy Thompson in Highlands, Matthews painted portraits of several Highlanders, including Dr. Thompson's wife, Helen McKinney Cleaveland Thompson (at left), when she was only 17. She is the Mama of her celebrated Highlands cookbook, *Mama's Recipes*. He also painted Charlie Wright, still famous four years after his death for his heroic rescue at Whiteside. (Portrait from Margaret McNeely Curtis.)

In the realm of powerful lyric poetry, Dr. Alfred Hawkins's daughter, Laura Hawkins (1861–1947), was known locally as the "Mountain Poet." As early as the 1880s, her poems sang of mountain trails, crags and glens, woodland fruits and forest flowers, birdsongs, the first gleam of morning, and the beauty of the stars. She basked in nature's joys and keenly suffered its losses. (Photograph from Dr. Larry Jason Hawkins.)

Often regarded as the poet laureate of Highlands, Bess Hines Harkins (1912–1986) revered the splendor and majesty of her mountains and waterfalls to the point of earning the title "Emily Dickinson of the Blue Ridge Mountains." The prose and poetry of "Bess the Woods Wanderer" from the late 1920s until the 1980s won numerous bicoastal awards for its beauty, spirit, and literary power. (Photograph from Sarah Harkins.)

Seven

THEN AND NOW

Viewed annually from mid-October to mid-November and again from mid-February to mid-March, the "Shadow of the Bear" is projected by Whiteside Mountain and Devil's Courthouse into Whiteside Cove around 5:30 to 5:45 in the evening and is best seen from Rhodes Big View on Highway 64 East between Highlands and Cashiers. The Cherokees saw it long ago even as Highlanders do now. (Photograph by the author, October 12, 2007, at 5:30 p.m.)

Through the millennia, the mountains, valleys, and waterfalls of the Highlands plateau have changed very little. Indeed, Highlands, with a current population of 958 year-round residents, remains a small town. To view the town from Sunset Rock is to realize clearly what anyone from New York or Miami or Atlanta grasps instantaneously: that Highlands is still a little village nestled in an ocean of mountain peaks blanketed with forests as far as the eye can see. What Henry Scadin photographed from Sunset Rock in 1907 (above) and hand-colored as a postcard is virtually identical to what visitors observe today (below). For change to be recognized in a small town like Highlands, it must be seen up close. An aerial then-and-now doesn't show significant change. (Above photograph by Henry Scadin from Hudson Library Collection; below photograph by the author.)

From Highlands's founding in 1875 until 1910, very little changed on Main Street. In 1910, from left to right above, were 1) Henry Skinner's (Hiram Paul's) double store, 2) open space, 3) Sinle Hood's quarters, 4) open space, 5) Potts Livery Stable, 6) open space, 7) Cleaveland's Grocery with gabled roof, 8) open space, 9) Bascom's Hardware, 10) Highlands House, and [right] Baxter White's store and post office. Today, from left to right below, are 1) Kent Limited and Juliana's, 2) Kilwin's, 3) post office building housing Village Kids and Suzette's, 4) Rice building housing Wit's End and Buck's Café, 5) Highlands Fine Art, 6) Cyrano's Bookshop, 7) Ann Jacob Gallery, 8) Trader Joe's, 9) Texaco Station, 10) Highlands Inn, and (right) Town Square. (Above photograph by Henry Scadin from Hudson Library Collection; below photograph by the author.)

Main Street East was a dirt road until crushed stone was applied in 1942. In the 1890 photograph by Scadin above, Dr. O'Farrell had his drug store in James Rideout's building to the left of Highlands House (right). The Altitude Oak, which stood in front of Highlands House as a symbol of the town since before its founding, bore a small plaque announcing Highlands's average altitude as 4,118 feet for the highest incorporated town in eastern America. It was felled in 1938 for the progress of pavement. Central House is today's Madison's Restaurant and the Rock Store the first floor of today's Old Edwards Inn. The deep swag in Main Street beyond Fourth Street intersection was filled in 1895 so that Main Street today (below) is relatively level. (Above photograph from Harbison Collection; below photograph by the author.)

When Kelsey and Hutchinson stood on Satulah Mountain in 1875 and visualized a town on the plateau below, they reckoned an east-west line (Main Street) bisected by a north-south line (Fourth Street). North Fourth Street crossed Mill Creek where Kelsey and William Soper built a bridge in 1877 (above in 1906). In 1886, a new bridge replaced the first one, and a pond was created for John Jay Smith's sawmill across the road. The new bridge was built, according to Joel Teague, with the aid of an old-time Georgia tonic that took the edge off working in the cold spring water of Highlands. By 1906, Will Cleaveland had erected his planing and blacksmith shop (above) where SweeTreats of Mountain Brook Center exists today. (Above photograph from Hudson Library Collection; below photograph by the author.)

Like Fourth Street North, Fourth Street South was sparsely populated for the first 50 years of Highlands's existence. Where C. L. Martin had his meat market in 1883 and Thoren Walden his drugstore in 1885, Billy Potts had his post office for one year in 1917 (above), next to what had once been Annie Dimick's Cheap Cash hardware store, site of today's Stone Lantern (below). Not until 1935 did Highlands have its first caution light at this corner and in 1947 its first stoplight, which was such a new concept at the time that the device had signs attached, explaining the three lights to the driving public: green for go, yellow for caution, and red for stop, with elaborate instructions regarding each. (Above photograph from Hudson Library Collection; below photograph by the author.)

INDEX

Visit us at
arcadiapublishing.com